Cambridge Elements ≡

Elements in Business Strategy
edited by
J.-C. Spender
Kozminski University

BEHAVIORAL STRATEGY

Exploring Microfoundations of Competitive Advantage

Nicolai J. Foss
Copenhagen Business School

Ambra Mazzelli
SKEMA Business School, Université Côte d'Azur (GREDEG)

Libby Weber
University of California

CAMBRIDGE
UNIVERSITY PRESS

CAMBRIDGE
UNIVERSITY PRESS

Shaftesbury Road, Cambridge CB2 8EA, United Kingdom

One Liberty Plaza, 20th Floor, New York, NY 10006, USA

477 Williamstown Road, Port Melbourne, VIC 3207, Australia

314–321, 3rd Floor, Plot 3, Splendor Forum, Jasola District Centre,
New Delhi – 110025, India

103 Penang Road, #05–06/07, Visioncrest Commercial, Singapore 238467

Cambridge University Press is part of Cambridge University Press & Assessment,
a department of the University of Cambridge.

We share the University's mission to contribute to society through the pursuit of
education, learning and research at the highest international levels of excellence.

www.cambridge.org
Information on this title: www.cambridge.org/9781009566773

DOI: 10.1017/9781009566759

When citing this work, please include a reference to the DOI 10.1017/9781009566759

First published 2024

A catalogue record for this publication is available from the British Library

ISBN 978-1-009-56677-3 Hardback
ISBN 978-1-009-56674-2 Paperback
ISSN 2515-0693 (online)
ISSN 2515-0685 (print)

Behavioral Strategy

Exploring Microfoundations of Competitive Advantage

Elements in Business Strategy

DOI: 10.1017/9781009566759
First published online: December 2024

Nicolai J. Foss
Copenhagen Business School

Ambra Mazzelli
SKEMA Business School, Université Côte d'Azur (GREDEG)

Libby Weber
University of California

Author for correspondence: Nicolai J. Foss, njf.si@cbs.dk

Abstract: Behavioral strategy has emerged as one of the most important currents in contemporary strategic management. But, what is it? Where does it come from? Why is it important? This Element provides a review of key streams in behavioral strategy, interpreting it as a consistently microfoundational approach to strategy that is grounded in evidence-based insight in behaviors and interaction. We show that there is considerable room for furthering the microfoundations of behavioral strategy and point to research opportunities and methods that may realize this aim. The Element is of interest to strategy scholars in general, and to PhD students in strategy research in particular.

Keywords: behavioral strategy, psychology-based microfoundations, managerial and organizational cognition, bounded rationality, competitive advantage

ISBNs: 9781009566773 (HB), 9781009566742 (PB), 9781009566759 (OC)
ISSNs: 2515-0693 (online), 2515-0685 (print)

Contents

Nothing is more fundamental in setting our research agenda and informing our research methods than our view of the nature of the human beings whose behavior we are studying

— Simon, Human Nature in Politics: The Dialogue
of Psychology with Political Science

1 Introduction and Overview

Behavioral Strategy and This Element

What is behavioral strategy? Where does it come from? Why is it important? One approach to answer these questions is to perform a little thought experiment. Imagine you are a high-level manager in the 1960s. Having attended business school (of which there were much fewer than now) you possess a highly diverse toolbox, derived from different disciplines, such as psychology, mathematics, political science, and economics. Yet when attempting to use these diverse tools, you soon realize they are based on widely different underlying assumptions about managers and employees, making them both incompatible and variably applicable in the real world. For example, the principles of negotiation you were taught, drawing on psychology and political science, are helpful in your managerial role in the company. In contrast, the economic principles you learned provide qualitative market- or industry-level predictions (Machlup, 1967), but are less useful for addressing many other issues you face as a manager. In economics, managers (like you) are assumed to be highly rational instantaneously choosing profit-maximizing input combinations. In practice, you know (too well) that managers are not capable of this.

In the face of managerial realities – complexity, limited information, political conflict, competing motivations, uncertainty, ill-defined goals, and power struggles – the need for strategy tools built on more realistic behavioral assumptions became apparent. Pioneering scholars in the field of strategy – Herbert A Simon (1948), Edith Penrose (1959), Alfred Chandler (1962), Richard Cyert and James G March (1963) – recognized that sound strategic management theory needs to come to grips with this reality. Thus, the field of strategy that emerged in the 1960s viewed managers as *boundedly rational* – that is, incapable of processing all available information, and therefore likely to make suboptimal decisions if evaluated through the lens of perfect rationality. With this auspicious start, one may expect strategy scholars to have made great strides in the understanding of boundedly rational managerial behavior, and at the very least to take great care in specifying behavioral assumptions about managerial behavior. However, much (perhaps most) strategy theory has not done this. Instead, the field became preoccupied with macro-level concepts such as industry or resource analysis, firm routines, capabilities, or competencies, and, more recently, with business models and ecosystems (Felin & Foss, 2005). As a result, most strategy theorizing leaves assumptions about individuals unspecified and opaque.

In this Element, we delve into the field of behavioral strategy, which attempts to address this theoretical blindspot by using evidence-based behavioral assumptions as the foundation of strategic thinking. We see behavioral strategy as *microfoundational*: it seeks to ground theorizing (and explanation and prediction) in individuals and their interactions. Thus, instead of building theory around an organizational actor, who merely has limited information processing capacity, this research also assumes individuals have a variety of motivations and emotions, use heuristics, and are subject to cognitive biases. Yet, after surveying the research in behavioral strategy, we see that these intentions have only been partially fulfilled, and further, not all of what passes as behavioral strategy is actually microfoundational. Thus, a key purpose of this Element is to uncover the substantial "microfoundational potential" that remains untapped within the field of behavioral strategy.

A second key objective of the Element is to present the diversity of behavioral strategy research. A significant part of this tradition is rooted in the already well-researched behavioral theory of the firm (Cyert & March, 1963), which addresses firms' responses to performance deviations from "aspiration levels" (basically, their quantified goals). As a result, scholars less acquainted with behavioral strategy typically equate the subfield with this perspective. Yet, many other streams of behavioral strategy research have developed more recently. By exposing readers to this work, we hope to demonstrate the diversity of behavioral strategy research, and inspire others to take up these novel research threads and weave them into an even more vibrant behavioral strategy tapestry than that created only with the behavioral theory of the firm.

The Relevance of a Behavioral Approach to Strategic Decisions

To start our journey into behavioral strategy, we need to go back to the very definition of "strategy" itself. A "strategy" is an action plan chosen by general management that allows an organization to create and capture value over an extended time period in a way that builds on the strengths of the organization (e.g., Chandler, 1962; Rumelt, 1979). Since the 1960s, academics, consultants, and gurus have devised diagnostic and analytical frameworks to aid in strategy formulation and implementation. Yet, these tools often overlook the boundedly rational nature of managers and the psychological influences at play.

Take, for example, Michael Porter's (1980) well-known Five Forces framework, a staple in strategy courses. It analyzes industry profit potential as driven by intraindustry rivalry, supplier and customer bargaining power, as well as the competitive threats posed by potential entrants and substitutes. In developing their firm's strategy, managers are urged to take these forces into account and shield against them. There are several tacit psychological assumptions in this strategy development process, which remain that way because decision-making and decision-makers are not explicitly discussed in most presentations of the framework. Specifically, the framework implicitly assumes managers possess a uniform cognitive representation (or "mental model") of the industry and complete information on various market elements like customers' willingness to pay, supplier costs, and competitive motivations and actions. This overlooks the reality that managers may hold different interpretations of the same industry, even if they conduct a Five Forces analysis.

As both a research field and an emerging managerial practice, behavioral strategy is fundamentally about making these implicit psychological assumptions explicit by exploring the intersection of psychology and strategy to understand and improve strategic decision-making. While the field of psychology uses the term "behavioral" to mean "behaviorist," echoing the stimulus-response theories of Pavlov and Skinner, this term takes on a distinctly different meaning in the field of strategy. Introduced in 2010 by Fox and Lovallo during their consulting work for McKinsey, behavioral strategy simply means "Strategy + Psychology."

The importance of adding psychology to strategy in today's world cannot be overstated, as recent events highlighted how it shapes decision-making and outcomes. For example, financial decision-makers' cognitive biases and herd behavior contributed to the 2008 financial crisis. Similarly, social influences and behavioral biases among individual investors drove the recent GameStop stock market frenzy.

Historical examples abound, but the Covid-19 pandemic and the disruptions it induced in the global economy clearly underscore the importance of understanding how decision-makers interpret and adapt to major disturbances that produce deeply complex, highly uncertain strategic problems. To most decision-makers, the pandemic was a "black swan" in the sense of Taleb (2007): an unknown (or at least something very much out of the ordinary) with massive negative consequences that required extensive sensemaking. For medical and health decision-makers, uncertainty was rampant, including the dynamics of the spread of the disease, the spatial variation in incidence, the epidemiological parameters, the role of superspreaders, and so on. Governments faced ambiguities about Covid-19's economic impact, the set of possible policy actions, and the outcomes of such actions under different scenarios (Ehrig & Foss, 2020). Corporate decision-makers also faced uncertainties regarding end markets, supply chains, and workforce consequences. Their responses differed markedly. For example, while most containerized shipping companies cut back on tonnage, one of the world's biggest operators, Danish Maersk did not, dramatically increasing its earnings when the pandemic's influence on trade patterns turned out to be less severe than anticipated (Maersk, 2023).

Most policy decision-making during the pandemic was characterized by "novelty, complexity and open-endedness" (Mintzberg et al., 1976: 250), and, initially, a lack of clarity on how to respond (Foss, 2020). However, countries that had recently experienced major influenza-like epidemics (e.g., Taiwan) quickly implemented preventive measures. In other words, prior experience played a major role in how rapidly actors could react and how much search was required among available responses. The observed response patterns suggest the presence of anchoring effects stemming from, for example, dramatic footage of global spots that were particularly hard hit by the pandemic outbreak. They also showcase confirmation bias supporting the choice of such reference points and leading to escalation of commitment to the chosen courses of action. While the pandemic prompted policymakers to implement a range of measures to contain the spread of the virus and mitigate its impact on public health and the economy, the global political response to the crisis was chaotic, fragmented, and often myopic, which led some policymakers to delay or underfund public health interventions, such as testing and contact tracing, in favor of measures that had more immediate effects, such as lockdowns. Governments tried to muddle through in the face of uncertainty by imitating each other (Sebatu et al., 2020). In sum, the Covid-19 pandemic certainly highlighted the crucial role of psychology in shaping strategic decision-making and outcomes, particularly under uncertainty. Behavioral strategy (Powell, Lovallo, & Fox, 2011) is vital in the broader world today, as suggested by the fact that psychological explanations are often invoked in explaining overall firm behavior and outcomes in both the popular business press (*Forbes, Fortune*, etc.), newspapers (*Wall Street Journal, Financial Times*), and magazines (*Harvard Business Review, Sloan Management Review, McKinsey Quarterly*). Additionally, well-known business failures (such as those of Blockbuster, Kodak, and Polaroid) that are a staple in MBA teaching, are at least partially attributed to senior managers' cognitive limitations constraining the development of organizational capabilities and, ultimately, adaptation (e.g., Tripsas & Gavetti, 2000). Given their frequency, these explanations further underscore the need for research-driven inquiries into these psychological aspects of firm performance.

What Is "Behavioral Strategy"?

There is a long tradition in strategy research of drawing on psychology (especially cognitive psychology, which is very roughly the study of how people think). But as already suggested the increasingly turbulent business and social environment has underscored the relevance and explanatory power of behavioral strategy research, as it is uniquely positioned to shed light on decision-making in environments characterized by high levels of uncertainty (Cyert & March, 1963), complexity (Busenitz & Barney, 1997), and urgency (Forbes, 2005). Specifically, behavioral strategy research draws on psychological theories and concepts – such as cognitive biases, emotions, motivations, and social influences – to understand how firms obtain and sustain competitive advantage (or, fail to achieve such advantage). This understanding helps managers and employees make decisions and take actions that enable their organizations to adapt to new challenges, sustain their performance, and ensure long-term survival. As such, it represents a vital area of inquiry for scholars and practitioners alike who seek to better understand the complexities of today's world and help organizations thrive in the face of uncertainty. It is thus not surprising that behavioral strategy research is an increasingly important voice in the strategy field, especially following its institutionalization as a distinct subfield in 2013: the founding of the Behavioral Strategy Interest Group in the Strategic Management Society.

Yet, the field of strategy has not always been open to studying behavioral strategy. To underscore the importance of including cognitive biases in strategic decision-making research, Lovallo and Sibony (2010) worked with McKinsey & Company to conduct a survey of 2,207 executives about the quality of strategic decision-making inside organizations. About 60 percent of respondents indicated that good and bad decisions occur with equal frequency, while 13 percent noted that good decisions were very infrequent. Probing into the reasons for this skepticism, the survey further examined the role of detailed analysis versus the structure of decision-making processes. The results revealed that decision process structure was six times more influential on decision quality than the depth of analysis. That is not to say analysis is unimportant. But, it highlights that a biased decision process can undermine even the most thorough analysis. Additionally, they discovered that implementing practices to debias decision-making could improve a company's ROI by 6.9 percent, demonstrating the tangible benefits of high-quality decision-making.

While behavioral strategy is receiving increasing recognition and acceptance, there is still disagreement as to how to define this subfield. Powell, Lovallo, and Fox (2011: 1371) offered the following definition of behavioral strategy:

> Behavioral strategy merges cognitive and social psychology with strategic management theory and practice. Behavioral strategy aims to bring realistic assumptions about human cognition, emotions, and social behavior to the strategic management of organizations and, thereby, to enrich strategy theory, empirical research, and real-world practice.

Other definitions of behavioral strategy have followed, either narrowing or expanding the subfield's scope (see Gavetti, 2012; Hambrick & Crossland, 2018). A comparably narrow definition provided by Levinthal (2011) suggests that a behavioral approach to strategy involves systematically building from the idea of a "cognitive representation" of a decision problem (Levinthal, 2011: 1519). Gavetti (2012) also refers to behavioral strategy as "the psychological underpinnings of a given phenomenon, where psychological broadly denotes 'being about mental process'" (Gavetti, 2012: 267). On the other hand, Rindova et al. (2012) adopts a broad "socio-cognitive perspective" focusing on "the roles of managers' and observers' attention; the bounded rationality of their cognitions, intuitions, and emotions; and the use of biases and heuristics to socially construct 'perceptual answers' to traditional strategic management questions about how firms obtain and sustain competitive advantage" (Pfarrer et al., 2019: 768). Finally, Hambrick and Crossland make a distinction between behavioral strategy "tents" of varying sizes. The small tent interpretation "amounts to a direct transposition of the logic of behavioral economics (and behavioral finance) to the field of strategic management," while the large tent conception includes "all forms and styles of research that consider *any* psychological, social, or political ingredients in strategic management" (2018: 25). However, the tent size favored by Hambrick and Crossland views behavioral strategy as a "commitment to understanding the psychology of strategists," which falls in the middle.

As illustrated by these diverse views of behavioral strategy, many disagreements remain around the *definition* of behavioral strategy, its *current scope* (what it seeks to explain and how it explains it), and its *boundaries* (what is behavioral strategy proper amidst the huge literature that makes use of psychology for theorizing about organizations and strategies). Despite these disagreements, most understandings of this subfield anchor on Herbert A. Simon's work and, more specifically, on the concept of bounded rationality.

Bounded rationality emerged from Simon's field studies of decision processes in local government bureaus. In contrast to classical economics models of perfect rationality, he observed that individuals are not capable of making optimal decisions. Bounded rationality posits that decision-making is influenced by a range of cognitive and environmental factors, including incomplete information, time constraints, and computational limitations that, in turn, make individuals satisfice rather than maximize (i.e., select courses of action that are satisfactory – rather than optimal) (Simon, 1955). Simon was explicitly committed to *microfoundations*, that is, the idea that we should seek to understand the characteristics and behaviors of aggregate social entities (such as organizations) in a manner that takes account of the nature and behavior of the individuals composing them

(Simon, 1991; Felin, Foss, & Ployhart, 2015). He was also committed to the notion that the study of decision-making must be *evidence-based* (Simon, 1978). Given that Simon's work is the commonality across inceptions of behavior strategy, we propose a definition of behavioral strategy based on these Simonian methodological commitments, which also provides shared ground between the existing definitions:

> **Definition**: *Behavioral strategy is the body of thought that addresses strategic management issues (e.g., CEO and top management team behaviors, entry decisions, competitive interaction, firm heterogeneity) in a way that: 1) is microfoundational, 2) embraces a psychology-based understanding of the actions and interactions of individuals to explain exchange or firm-level strategy phenomena, and 3) grounds theorizing in realistic and robust evidence about behaviors and interaction (rather than mathematical tractability, elegance, or convenience).*

Thus, behavioral strategy reinforces other influences that have shaped strategy research over the last few decades, particularly the increased emphasis on microfoundations (Felin & Foss, 2005; Felin et al., 2015) and on empirical methods that go beyond the regression-based analysis of archival data, as they do not allow for testing of underlying mechanisms. Behavioral strategy inherently requires mixed-methods approaches, involving various kinds of experimental and qualitative methodologies.

Themes and Currents in Behavioral Strategy

Simon's notion of bounded rationality imprinted much of the subsequent psychology-based strategy literature, including what we consider today to be behavioral strategy. Figure 1 provides a visual summary of the major contributions in the behavioral strategy field, grouping them into major research traditions. These traditions are plotted based on the most commonly adopted psychological constructs impacting strategy outcome variables and the level at which a construct is theorized within each tradition (i.e., microlevel (individual), meso-level (group), and macro-level (organization)).[1] This figure thus acts as a roadmap of the behavioral strategy subfield, as well as of Sections 2–4 in this Element.

Building on Simon's Bounded Rationality

As noted earlier, one traditional theme in behavioral strategy research hinges on premises that date back to Richard Cyert and James March's book *A Behavioral*

---

[1] To identify the major literature streams and contributions in the behavioral strategy landscape in Figure 1, we reviewed articles published in the most prominent management review journals, *Academy of Management Annals* and *Journal of Management* and retrieved literature review

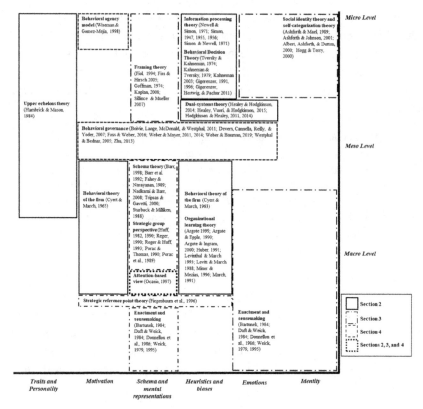

Figure 1 Major contributions in the behavioral strategy field

Theory of the Firm (1963) – a truly foundational contribution in terms of the inspiration it has provided behavioral strategy scholars (and strategy scholars in general). In their behavioral theory of the firm (BTOF), Cyert and March (1963) follow Simon in explicitly criticizing neoclassical economics, specifically the neoclassical theory of the firm (i.e., the basic iso-cost and iso-quant curve apparatus taught in basic microeconomics). The inspiration for key parts of their theory is explicitly drawn from Simon. Rationality in BTOF is best understood in terms of *satisficing aspiration levels*, which may be thought of as the smallest acceptable outcomes for a goal, the line between perceived

---

articles containing the combination of the terms "strategy" AND "behavior" AND "psychology." This search yielded 1,732 results. We then manually inspected and screened this set of review articles to ensure that they mentioned psychology constructs and featured theoretical and empirical articles focused on firm-level behavior and/or outcomes, leading to thirty-one review articles. Hence, we examined the text and reference list of each of these articles to identify relevant theoretical traditions and plot them and some of their foundational studies in the behavioral strategy landscape. For illustrative purposes, we aggregated the psychological concepts into higher-level categories.

successes and failures, or as rules for simplifying evaluations (Greve, 1998). Moreover, *quasi-resolution of conflict* and *priority rules* govern which goal is addressed. Furthermore, firms are assumed to (only) act when they face a problem – when performance falls below an aspiration level – by searching for a solution. Additionally, similar to goal selection and performance assessment, this search is governed by rules (March & Simon, 1958), specifying the proximity of search to the problem, the current state of the organization, and vulnerable areas inside of it. Thus, search is problemistic, "simple-minded" (governed by simple models of causality), path-dependent (based on organizational history and accumulated knowledge embedded in the standard operating procedures and routines of the organization), and reflective of managerial preferences and employees' training and experience. From a methodological standpoint, *A Behavioral Theory of the Firm* commits to developing process-oriented models of the firm and linking them to the empirical world through decision-making simulations. As a result, this simulation approach has become a key tool for understanding and deriving nonobvious implications in subsequent behavioral theory of the firm research (Gavetti et al., 2012; Puranam et al., 2015).

Another traditional behavioral strategy research area directly descending from Cyert and March's theory (1963) is organizational learning research (Argote, 1999; Levit & March, 1988; Argote & Greve, 2007) which examines how organizations, seen as complex adaptive systems (Denrell & March, 2001), learn and draw inferences from experience (Levitt & March, 1988). Local (myopic) search is assumed as the main mechanism driving learning, resulting in suboptimal outcomes (Levinthal & March, 1993). These studies typically rely on agent-based simulation models, including NK models and bandit models, characterizing choices of action as existing on performance landscapes (Levinthal, 1997).

Another closely related traditional research stream builds on Cyert and March's rule-based view of organizational decision-making to examine the implications of decision rules for a series of organizational processes and outcomes, including learning (Lant & Mezias, 1992), adaptation (Lant, 1992), innovation (Mezias & Glynn, 1993), and performance. Adjacent to these contributions, is the view that organizational routines perform the double role of (1) providing stability and encapsulating firm-specific knowledge (Nelson & Winter, 1982), and (2) generating organizational change (Feldman & Pentland, 2003). This work augments March and Simon's (1958) and Cyert and March's conceptualization of routines as abstract and stable patterns shaping and guiding organizational behavior with human agency – organizational members' doings and acts – to introduce changes to routines, and therefore organizational change and performance.

While we will refer to these foundational contributions and their direct descendants several times in the subsequent sections, because of their centrality and extraordinary influence in the organization sciences, they have already been the subject of excellent reviews by Argote and Greve (2006) (Carnegie's School tradition), Baumann et al. (2019) (search in performance landscapes), Gavetti et al. (2007) (Carnegie's School tradition), Gavetti et al. (2012) (behavioral theory of the firm), Posen et al. (2018) (problemistic search), and Puranam et al. (2015) (bounded rationality).

However, as Figure 1 illustrates, behavioral strategy research encompasses more than these traditional streams, so we focus on the many other parts of behavioral strategy that explore topics beyond search and organizational learning, including, for example, Kahneman and Tversky's (1974, 1982) research on heuristics and biases (Section 2), the distinction between "hot" and "cold" cognition (e.g., Hodgkinson & Healey, 2011) (Section 2), Weick's thinking on managerial and organizational cognition (Weick, 1979) (Section 3), and work based on cognitive or motivational psychological theories, such as regulatory focus theory (e.g., Weber & Mayer, 2011) (Section 4). We delve into each of these sections in more detail below.

Information Processing, Heuristics, and Biases

In the second section, we present work on microlevel biases and heuristics that build on the notion of bounded rationality (continuous-line-patterned areas in Figure 1). It originates from two major individual-level research traditions that predict organizational decision-making: information-processing research (Simon & Newell, 1971) and behavioral decision research (Tversky & Kahneman, 1974; Kahneman & Tversky, 1979). Information processing research concerns human problem-solving and heuristics and views the decision-making process as a key unit of analysis (Simon & Newell, 1971). In particular, organizational behavior is explained by the discrepancy between the real world and the simplified model of reality in the human mind (Simon, 1955).

In behavioral decision research, bounded rationality leads humans to make fast decisions that produce systematic biases (or cognitive illusions). This research stream aimed to create an evidence-based map of bounded rationality "by exploring the systematic biases that separate the beliefs that people have and the choices they make from the optimal beliefs and choices assumed in rational-agent models" (Kahneman, 2003: 1449). According to the two main exponents of this stream, Amos Tversky and Daniel Kahneman, fast thinking manifests itself in decision-makers relying on rules of thumb (heuristics) – such as representativeness, availability, and anchoring and adjustment – which lead to systematic divergences from the normative models of behavior in classical economic theories. Still lying within the behavioral decision research tradition but promoting a fundamentally different view of heuristics is the work on fast-and-frugal heuristics (Gigerenzer et al., 1999; Gigerenzer, Hertwig, & Pachur 2011). Here, humans are seen as intuitive statisticians, who can adopt heuristics in a way that increases accuracy and minimizes effort, achieving what is defined as ecological rationality. Another important extension of behavioral decision research is represented by the dual-systems theory of cognition (Chaiken & Trope, 1999). This theory builds on Kahneman and Tversky view's of decision-making as dominated by two systems: a system that operates through largely automatic, preconscious processes involving the development of heuristics; and one that operates via more effortful, deeper, and analytical processes. Yet, in contrast to Kahneman and Tversky's view of automatic thinking to be seen as the default mode and the main source of systematic biases, researchers in this stream view the two systems as operating simultaneously and emphasize the importance of humans' capability to switch back and forth between these two processes depending on situational circumstances (Hodgkinson & Healey, 2011).

Interpretive Perspectives

The third section addresses the stream of work exploring enactment and the related notion of sensemaking (dashed-dotted-patterned areas in Figure 1) – which has received substantial attention (e.g., Hodgkinson, 1997; Walsh, 1995). This stream challenges the notion of bounded rationality and its positivistic view of the world as an objective entity. In contrast, scholars belonging to this stream maintain a view of the environment as *enacted* – that is, socially constructed via a process of sensemaking through which individuals develop meaning from ambiguous environmental cues via local action, in turn, giving rise to even radically different perceptions of the business environment. Research in this interpretive stream can further be grouped into three traditions: micro- and meso-level work on schema and mental maps (Huff, 1982, 1990; Porac et al., 1989), micro- and meso-level work on social identity and identification (Ashforth & Mael, 1989; Albert, Ashforth, & Dutton, 2000); and meso- and macro-level work on enactment and sensemaking (Daft & Weick, 1984). The first sheds light on managers' cognitive mapping process (Hodgkinson et al., 2004), the content of these maps (Porac et al., 1995; Reger & Huff, 1993), and their implications for strategic decisions (e.g., Barr et al., 1992). It also provides insight into diver-gences between managers' cognitive maps and aggregation issues. The second tradition illuminates organizational members' social identity construction and its impact on the firm (Ashforth & Mael, 1989). The third stream focuses on the sensemaking process through which organizational members, when faced with disruptive events, collectively construct meaning and continue to enact the environment (Weick, 1995). Therefore, in contrast to the first stream, which assumes that a frame of meaning (or cognitive map) is already in place, and one needs to connect a new cue to the existing frame (through the act of mapping), the second stream is more concerned with the "invention" of a new frame. In this section, we shed insight into the distinctive facets of this stream's constitutive research traditions. We also discuss the difficulties of studying the mental representations and sensemaking processes of the organization's top management team members.

Behavioral Governance

In the fourth section of the Element, we focus on the motivation-related part of the behavioral strategy landscape in Figure 1 (dashed-patterned areas), and, specifically, on the behavioral governance traditions. Work in this tradition aims at augmenting corporate governance theories (i.e., agency theory; Fama & Jensen, 1983; Jensen & Meckling, 1976) and transaction cost economics (TCE; Williamson, 1975, 1985) with psychological theories and concepts to predict organizational outcomes, with a special focus on the role of governance – that is, "the formal structures, informal structures, and processes that exist in oversight roles and responsibilities in a corporate context" (Hambrick, Werder, & Zajac, 2008: 381) – in supporting cooperation among firms' internal and external constituents (Westphal & Zajac, 2013). In particular, work in this stream can be organized into three separate streams differing on the context of application, in terms of the "main agent(s)" to which they apply: (1) corporate leaders; (2) organizational members and employees; and (3) external stakeholders. Work focusing on corporate leaders examines executives' behaviors, as guided by self-interest and personal risk preferences and characterized by bounded rationality, and how certain incentives (e.g., equitable compensation), structures, and systems, by acting on executives' intrinsic, extrinsic motivation, and prosocial motivations can channel executives' efforts in directions that contribute positively to organizational and/or societal outcomes (Devers, Cannella, Reilly, & Yoder, 2007).

Research in the second stream explores how different organizational designs induce different motivations, leading to specific types of opportunism or cooperation (Weber, Foss, & Lindenberg, 2023), as well as specific transaction costs (Foss & Weber, 2016). Finally, work in the third stream examines how contract frames impact employees' regulatory focus, emotions, perceptions, and behaviors (Weber & Mayer, 2011), inducing desired exchange behaviors (Weber, Mayer, & Macher, 2011) and impacting the relationship between firms.

This section also builds on the second and third sections to examine efficient transaction governance decisions that take different organizational cognitive frames into account (Weber & Mayer, 2014).

Research Challenges in Behavioral Strategy

In the final section of the Element (Section 5), we present the major research challenges in behavioral strategy research and propose a roadmap to advance research in this field. We focus on definitional and methodological issues. From a definitional standpoint, we describe how existing behavioral strategy research has largely overlooked possible implications of branches of psychology beyond cognition (cf. Gigerenzer & Goldstein, 1996), such as emotions, affect, intuition, and even motivation. Because of these tendencies, we note that there is a huge potential for future behavioral strategy research that has not yet been tapped, for example, examining the impact of strategic beliefs on firm performance, or the psychology of goals (Lindenberg & Foss, 2011), or motivational psychology, and how these aspects influence firm value creation. We also present potential issues with the widespread approach of anthropomorphizing organizations. From a methodological standpoint, we discuss the potential benefits of methodological pluralism to capture and account for the complex dynamics of real organizational settings.

2 Bounded Rationality, Heuristics, and Biases: From Simon to Computational Models

Introduction

While bounded rationality is foundational to most management thought, it is particularly important in a behavioral strategy context. A key purpose of this section is to trace thinking on bounded rationality from its earliest history in Simon (1947) through the heuristics and biases program of Kahneman and Tversky (1974) to modern computational approaches and ecological rationality. As such, the section lays the foundations for subsequent sections. However, along the way, we will also note various limitations in the way behavioral strategy has dealt with bounded rationality, such as a tendency to reify the concept, specifically, move it to the organizational level without considering the aggregation process.

Bounded Rationality: Simon's Grand Theme

From "Perfect" to "Bounded" Rationality

As its name suggests, bounded rationality was coined as a critique of the assumption of "perfect" rationality. Extreme assumptions often serve science well, and, arguably, the assumption of perfect rationality has, in many ways, served economics well, as it furthers tractability (i.e., decision problems can be represented as maximization problems), tends to lead to unique predictions (given certain assumptions on the maximization problem) and is not completely unrealistic (e.g., when a decision situation is sufficiently simple). And yet, the assumption has also been criticized for as long as it has been articulated (e.g., Veblen, 1898).

To understand what the critique is about, it is important to understand what the assumption entails and what it does not. Perfect rationality does not assume omniscience or perfect foresight. Economics has long since dispensed with those assumptions in favor of assumptions of "asymmetric and imperfect information." Thus, information and uncertainty or risk are included in the set of constraints on the decision problem, but decision-makers are nevertheless assumed to be capable of maximizing and arriving at the best possible solution. This view – further refined in the 40s and 50s in the works of von Neumann and Morgenstern (1944), Friedman and Savage (1948), and Luce and Raiffa (1957) – implicitly assumes that decision-makers have an unlimited capacity for processing the information they possess or acquire. Accordingly, any decision problem can potentially be addressed and handled immediately and perfectly.

If taken literally, it is easy to see how extreme this view is, as "there is a complete lack of evidence that, in actual human choice situations … these computations are in fact performed" (Simon, 1955: 104). Providing this evidence, and, more generally, understanding how decision-makers *actually* make decisions and if general principles can be constructed about such decision-making, was a significant part of the multi- and interdisciplinary *oeuvre* of Herbert A Simon.

Simon (1947) points out that although we may intend to be rational, we do not have the wits to calculate the optimal solution for many decision situations. In Simon's often-quoted phrase, we are *boundedly rational*: "intendedly rational, but limitedly so" (1947: 88). Of course, this is a negative definition in the sense that it tells us what bounded rationality is not rather than what it actually is (Foss, 2003). However, exploring what bounded rationality entails for individual decision-making and, in particular, in an organizational context, has constituted a central scholarly effort in a number of related but distinct research streams over the last seven decades. This includes work in information processing (Simon & Newell, 1971), within the broad Carnegie School (March & Simon, 1958) – including, the behavioral theory of the firm (Cyert & March, 1963), the attention-based view of the firm (Ocasio, 1997), and modern computational approaches that highlight the search and adaptation aspects of bounded rationality (Levinthal, 1997; Puranam et al., 2015) – as well as work on behavioral decision research from behavioral economics (Tversky & Kahneman, 1974; Kahneman & Tversky, 1979), top management teams (Ha0mbrick & Mason, 1984), and even TCE (Williamson, 1996; see Section 4). The first major advance in the bounded rationality program is the expansion to consider satisficing and search.

Bounded Rationality in Individual Decision-Making: Information Processing, Heuristics, and Satisficing Search

In his 1955 article, "A behavioral model of rational choice," Simon centers his critique around two fundamental assumptions inherent in rational decision theory, namely (1) perfect computational powers on the part of decision-makers and (2) the existence of a well-defined set of conceivable actions which lead to certain consequences that can all be evaluated and compared, thereby translating into a complete preference ordering and a unique optimal action.

In place of such unrealistic assumptions, Simon (1955, 1956) fundamentally redefines rationality from the "substantive" notion associated with standard economics to a more "procedural" notion (Simon, 1978), whereby "an explanation of an observed behavior of the organism is provided by a program of primitive information processes that generates this behavior" (Newell, Shaw, & Simon, 1958: 151). Thus, the attention turns to decision-making and problem-solving (or search in later work) processes as guided by "programs." In particular, when human beings are observed working on problems that are difficult but not unsolvable for them, their behaviors reveal basic properties that relate to how they process information, namely serial processing, small short-term memory, and infinite long-term memory with fast retrieval but slow storage (Simon & Newell, 1971). These properties impose strong constraints on how individuals can seek solutions to problems in large problem spaces (cf. Simon & Newell, 1971: 149). In these situations, regardless of how large the problem space is, heuristics direct problem solvers' attention to small, promising regions of the problem space or "a set of possible outcomes ... such that the pay-off is satisfactory ... for all these outcomes," while ignoring the rest, and to search around certain "behavior alternatives" until those "whose outcomes are all [in the set]" are identified (p.106). In other words, search involves refining the understanding of how actions map onto consequences in a sequential manner, which inherently depends on how information is embedded in problem spaces, extracted by heuristic processes, and used to guide search.

According to Simon, the simplest way to extract and use information for problem-solving is hill climbing. Using the heuristics of "always going upward," decision-makers try to identify alternatives that are associated with a higher performance payoff compared with the current one. The choice of an efficient next step is dictated by means-end analysis–a type of heuristics that allows a decision maker to find differences between already explored alternatives and a goal state (Simon & Newell, 1971). Therefore, search continues until an outcome that is "satisfactory" in terms of meeting the target is found (Simon, 1947). As Simon (1955: 114) explains, satisficing as a decision heuristic has the advantage of being "computationally manageable," and at the same intuitively realistic.

In this sense, Simon's theory of decision-making is primarily a theory describing problem-solving programs and their role in making the decision-maker, as an information-processing system, adapt to the task environment (i.e., the objective problem space). Such a focus embeds a quest for generalizability and parsimony to make the theory applicable to a variety of problem situations as well as allowing for examination via mathematical and computational modeling. Indeed, as we discuss in the next section, Simon's work inspired the development of an entire research program relying strongly on formal (mathematical and computational) modeling to describe and analyze the processes of search and adaptation in organizations (Puranam et al., 2015).

Moving Bounded Rationality into the Firm: Problemistic Search and Attention

From Cyert and March to Computational Models

Although Simon's (1947) concern with bounded rationality emerged from his close study (for his Ph.D. thesis) of decision-making in a public bureau, much of his early work on the topic, including his multiple collaborations with Alan Newell, mainly considers individual decision-making. Instead, the concept of satisficing search was extended to the organizational level by Cyert and March in their landmark 1963 book, *A Behavioral Model of the Firm*. As mentioned in Section 1, the most important elaboration of the book is the notion of problemistic search, that is search triggered by negative divergences between realized performance and aspiration levels (acceptable performance thresholds set by a dominant coalition of boundedly rational decision-makers through quasi-resolution of conflict (see Posen et al., 2020 for a review)). In doing so, Cyert and March emphasized the importance of feedback in guiding search (which had also appeared in Simon 1966).

Since Cyert and March (1963), a substantial number of papers have been published following a basic scheme in which: (1) agents are equipped with models of their environments, (2) representations inform the choices agents make, (3) these choices are "tested" in the relevant environment generating feedback, and (4) the representations in the environmental model are adapted, resulting in novel choices (see Puranam et al., 2015). This scheme underpins research on the behavioral theory of the firm, including research on the "exploitation-exploration tradeoff" (March, 1991) and work that uses "NK models," originally developed by theoretical biologist Stuart Kauffman (1993) and introduced to management research by Levinthal (1997).

Behavioral strategy using an NK model depicts organizations as moving on a "fitness landscape," an N-dimensional space that maps each attribute (characteristic or policy dimension of an organization) and its performance consequences. Crucially, the topology of the landscape is determined by the degree of interdependence (i.e., complementarity) between the attributes, K. That is, K measures how many other attributes influence a given attribute. While a small value of K implies few peaks in the landscape or just a single one (a "smooth landscape"), a high value indicates many peaks (a "rugged landscape"). Even though the landscape exists in objective reality, the organization does not know its topology and therefore has to engage in search, either local (i.e., only changing one attribute) or global ("long jumps"; changing all attributes). It is intuitive that if the landscape has just one peak, this peak will be reached through local search. In contrast, in a rugged landscape, organizations that engage in only local search may get stuck on local peaks. While this seems to make global search generally attractive, such search is more costly to engage in. Thus, organizational search behavior results from a tradeoff between the benefits and costs of the two types of search. This line of research has been thriving since the late 1990s (Gavetti & Levinthal, 2000; Puranam et al., 2015), percolating widely beyond the community of modelers and resulting in empirical work investigating the impact of negative performance feedback on the likelihood and intensity of organizational and strategic changes (e.g., Audia & Greve, 2006; Greve 1998). This stream of empirical research has also shown that, especially under conditions of uncertainty, decision-makers selectively imitate the actions of other firms (Rhee et al., 2006). In particular, to improve firm performance while avoiding the risks and costs of online search and experimentation, they learn vicariously by absorbing knowledge produced by other firms' explorations (Baum et al., 2000; Levitt & March, 1988).

From March and Simon to the Attention-Based View

Further implications of bounded rationality at the organizational level were added through work from Simon's collaboration with the political scientist James G. March and, more recently, by Ocasio's (1997) attention-based view of the firm. In Simon's (1948) original view, the main role of organizations was to structure the attention of individual decision-makers by offering both a physical and cognitive division of labor (member A works on problems of type Z, while B works on type Y problems, etc.) (Dearborn & Simon, 1958). In the book *Organizations*, March and Simon explicitly focus on providing a theory for when, where, and how organizations search for information about urgent problems, alternatives, and their consequences. More specifically, they illustrate that organizations structure and channel the allocation of cognitive effort and attention through the division and spatial allocation of labor, and decide which problems should be worked on based on "decision premises" (March & Simon, 1958). We will return to some of these aspects in Section 4.

Building on March and Simon (1958), Ocasio (1997) formulated the attention-based view of the firm in an article published almost four decades after their classic work. Ocasio interprets bounded rationality as individuals' limited attentional capacity. Attention is the "noticing, encoding, interpreting, and focusing of time and effort on issues (problems, opportunities, threats . . .) and answers (alternatives, projects, procedures, . . .)" (Ocasio, 1997: 188). A key purpose of organizations is therefore to direct attention in the best possible manner (Joseph & Gaba, 2020). While the main emphasis is on the attention of the firm's top decision-makers, Ocasio develops a more general theory that picks up on Simon (1947) and March and Simon (1958) in showing how organizations sculpt decisions by defining and allocating the stimuli that channel attention (cf. Ocasio, 2011). Thus, organizational problems ("Hey, demand dropped in market x," "Ugh, a machine broke down") in a specific unit selectively trigger the attention of that unit's employees.

Heuristics and Biases and Ecological Rationality

The Heuristics and Biases Program

A key theme in Simon's idea of bounded rationality is that decision-makers often rely on cognitive shortcuts because they lack the processing capacity to make fully informed decisions (Schwenk, 1984; Simon, 1956). Satisficing is one such heuristic, enabling decision-makers to economize on cognitive resources as compared to computationally more demanding approaches, such as maximizing. The downside is, of course, that decision-makers may choose and stick to inferior alternatives. This basic duality is central in the behavioral decision research initiated by the behavioral economists Tversky and Kahneman (1974) (see Kahneman (2003) for a summary), and often referred to as the heuristics and biases program (Kahneman, 2003, 2011; Kahneman & Tversky, 1979). Additionally, it is now seen as an important instance of "dual processing theory" which stresses the "twin imperative of having to process information deliberatively and in detail, but also being able to cut through such detail with minimal cognitive effort to perform tasks more efficiently" (Hodgkinson et al., 2023: 1042). Notably, the heuristics and biases program, albeit originating directly from Simon's bounded rationality notion, was framed as a new paradigm departing from "bounded rationality, satisficing, and simulations" through the reliance on empirical evidence – mainly of an experimental nature (Sent, 2004: 742).

The key idea in the heuristics and biases program is that the manifold heuristics that decision-makers utilize[2] are likely to result in a rich set of cognitive biases, rendering the decision-making process systematically flawed – at least if evaluated related to a perfect rationality ideal. The search for such biases has become a major industry, with the number of biases at 188 at last count.[3] While it is debatable how distinct many of these biases truly are (Oeberst & Imhoff, 2023), representativeness and availability biases, both stemming from the tendency to focus attention on supposedly typical features of a decision situation, are among the more well-known ones (Hodgkinson et al., 2023; Kiesler & Sproull, 1982). Other well-known biases (probably so well-known that an explanation is not necessary) are hindsight, self-serving, overconfidence, anchoring, and confirmation biases.

One of the most influential theories in this program is Kahneman and Tversky's (1979) prospect theory. Conceived as an alternative to expected utility theory, it provides a model for predicting individual decision-making under risk in contexts of isolated gambles characterized by simple choices with two clear prospects or alternatives and stated probabilities (Kahneman, 2003). The theory is based on the following three core assumptions: (1) decision-makers weigh assured outcomes more than probable outcomes, (2) they simplify decision-making by focusing on differences between choices rather than their commonalities, and (3) they tend to be risk-averse in the domain of (small) gains and risk-seeking in the domain of (small) losses. As a result, decision-makers prefer an assured gain over an uncertain gain with a marginally higher expected value and prefer an uncertain loss over an assured loss with a marginally lower expected value (Bromiley & Rau, 2022; Holmes et al., 2011).

Prospect theory has been very popular in strategy research (see e.g., Holmes et al., 2011; Hoskisson et al., 2017). It is typically applied to the top management team or the organization to explain the relationship between a firm's negative performance and its risk-taking (e.g., risky actions such as acquisitions, divestitures, and new product introductions). The application of prospect theory to firm strategic decisions has not come without criticism (Bromiley,

---

[2] Such as the *one ounce rule*, that is, continue searching as long as options improve; at the first downturn, stop searching and take the previous best option, or the default heuristic, that is, if there is a default, follow it, or imitate the majority or the successful).

[3] www.visualcapitalist.com/every-single-cognitive-bias/

2010; Bromiley & Rau, 2022). While prospect theory examines the behavior of an individual decision-maker confronted with a simple well-structured problem with clear prospects or alternatives and known probabilities, the problems organizations are confronted with are generally complex, collective, and involve a substantial level of uncertainty. Explicit examinations of the validity of prospect theory to predict individual choices in more complex contexts similar to organizational ones have provided far from reassuring results (e.g., Bromiley, 2010; Spiliopoulos & Hertwig, 2023).

This aggregation issue emerges in most strategy research building on the heuristics and biases program. Another example is the upper echelons research area founded by Hambrick and Mason (1984), who were early adopters of the heuristics and biases program (e.g., Barnes, 1984; Das & Teng, 1999) (see the review and discussion in Hodgkinson et al., 2023). In their foundational work and that built on it, executives' and senior managers' characteristics and traits were grafted onto behavioral theories of decision-making (cf. Hambrick, 2007) to show the heuristic nature of their decision-making and the possibly biased nature of the resulting firm-level strategic decisions and outcomes (e.g., Chen et al., 2015; Li & Tang, 2010; Wesley et al., 2022). As suggested, these studies tend to take an aggregate view without delving into how biases and heuristics may be either mitigated or accentuated by social interactions and dynamics between firm leaders. Moreover, the bulk of this work focuses primarily on top-manager overconfidence (Burkhardt et al., 2022), with Hodgkinson et al. (2023) identifying approximately 50 percent of published papers in this area addressing this particular bias.

In contrast to the work on decision-making in top management, even less attention has been paid to how heuristics and biases at lower organizational levels impact value creation. In one such application, Foss and Weber (2016) consider framing and social comparison biases that may arise in exchanges between members and units in firms. They argue that different hierarchical structures induce different biases, giving rise to predictable frictions in internal exchanges. Given that this line of research is very recent, this area represents a significant research opportunity in behavioral strategy.

Finally, Kahneman and Tversky's original goal "to obtain a map of bounded rationality" recently re-gained momentum in work examining individual-level beliefs and strategic choices (Kahneman, 2003) using neurocognitive experiments. To do so, a group of behavioral strategy scholars directly examine decision-makers' mental processes via brain imaging techniques (e.g., Laureiro-Martínez, Brusoni, & Zollo, 2010; Laureiro-Martínez, Brusoni, Canessa, & Zollo, 2015). While holding some promise, this approach may risk excessively detaching decision-making from its organizational context, thereby losing external validity (cf. Felin et al., 2015).

Moreover, the nature of brain imaging methodology may change the nature of the decision-making task, perhaps reducing its internal validity. We will return to some of these issues in the final section of the Element.

Ecological Rationality

Whereas most research in the heuristics and biases tradition emphasizes the downside of heuristics (i.e., biases), the ecological rationality program accentuates their upside. Picking up on Simon's (1955) idea, this approach focuses on the skilled application of heuristics by decision-makers. So in this research, a heuristic is seen as "a strategy with the goal of making decisions more quickly, frugally, and/or accurately than more complex methods" (Gigerenzer & Gassmeier, 2011). Strikingly, Gigerenzer and his co-authors show that heuristics are not second-best approximations to maximizing rationality, but may often lead to faster and better outcomes, particularly in uncertain, ambiguous environments with few useful data points (e.g., Gigerenzer & Gaissmaier, 2011). As with the neuroscience approach to behavioral strategy, the study of ecologically rational, fast, and frugal heuristics in organizations in general and in strategy in particular is still in its infancy. Pioneer work has been done by Bingham and Eisenhardt (2011), who studied the formation of heuristics during the internationalization processes of six technology-based ventures. However, except for Luan, Reb, and Gigerenzer (2019), there is still very little research examining the formation and use of heuristics at the firm level and their implications for organizational decision-making and strategic adaptation. Again, the dearth of research on this important topic represents an important opportunity for work in behavioral strategy.

Conclusion: Simon's Incomplete Revolution

This section briefly outlines the history of the evolution of bounded rationality originally proposed by Simon (1947). On one hand, the revolution around rationality, information processing, and behavior that Simon initiated has been exceedingly successful. As a result, the implications of bounded rationality have become increasingly concrete in such concepts as satisficing search (Simon, 1955), representations (March & Simon, 1958, discussed in Chapter 3), aspiration levels and problemistic search (Cyert & March, 1963), and limited attention (Ocasio, 1997). It is also more clear how it is embedded in an organizational context (Simon, 1947; March & Simon, 1958; Cyert & March, 1963; Ocasio, 1997), linked to top manager decision-making (Hambrick & Mason, 1984; Hodgkinson et al., 2023), articulated in terms of the competing heuristics and biases (Tversky & Kahneman, 1974) and ecological rationality

(Gigerenzer & Gassmeier, 2011), and formalized relying on modeling techniques like NK-modeling and other computational models (Puranam et al., 2015). In other words, bounded rationality evolved through refinement, extension, application, and formalization, which is how successful scientific ideas usually advance. Indeed, it is not amiss to suggest that bounded rationality is *the* way in which most management scholars view human rationality.

On the other hand, there is significant imprecision and inconsistency in the basic conceptualization and model of bounded rationality in management research, as well as its application to organizations and their strategies. A fundamental critique of this work (which does not apply to Simon's research) is that it focuses on errors rather than *success* of decision-making. As the ecological rationality critique implies, the heuristics and biases program itself is strongly representative of this tendency, but so too is bounded rationality research on, for example, the exploitation/exploration tradeoff (March, 1991). This critique also suggests that much bounded-rationality research implicitly accepts the standard optimization model as its normative benchmark – rationality is "bounded" relative to this benchmark (Foss, 2003). Indeed, formal treatments of bounded rationality make ample use of standard probabilistic reasoning (e.g., Kahneman, 2003), and some of the best-developed and most influential models of bounded rationality (notably, prospect theory, Kahneman & Tversky, 1979) are models that assume environments characterized by risk. However, strategy formulation and implementation often involve epistemic conditions to which probabilistic tools are less well suited, notably Knightian uncertainty (i.e., decision-makers do not confront a given state space, cannot place probabilities on outcomes, etc.). There are some obvious links, as, for example, the inability to put meaningful probabilities to outcomes or identify the full set of possible outcomes (both manifestations of Knightian uncertainty) may result from bounded rationality. But, at least so far bounded-rationality research has said little about decision-making and behaviors under uncertainty rather than risk (Mousavi & Gigerenzer, 2014). Furthermore, as Hodgkinson and Healey (2011) argue, most interpretations of bounded rationality in strategy are through the lens of "cold cognition." inherently downplaying the importance of affect and emotions.

Although research has made several significant advances in how bounded rationality is applied in the context of firm strategy, many aspects are still unclear in this research program. For instance, despite the importance and centrality of problemistic search in strategy research, how problem identification, diagnosis, and solving occur in an organization remains something of a black box (Posen et al., 2018). Additionally, while both March and Simon (1958) and Cyert and March (1963) theorized about how firms establish priorities in the presence of multiple goals and corresponding aspiration levels (e.g., different goals and aspiration levels for different units), empirical evidence of the mechanisms regulating the allocation of attention is scant (cf. Mazzelli et al., 2019). Moreover, while research distinguished between social and historical sources of aspiration levels, the mechanisms driving choices of such levels, including why particular social referents are chosen, remain less well understood.

More fundamentally, significant challenges remain in bringing bounded rationality to bear at all organizational levels, and not just the individual and the dominant coalition or top management team levels (Hambrick, 2007). Indeed, bounded rationality is an individual-level construct developed from the observation of decision-makers solving rather simple problems in controlled environments – as was the case for several of the constructs in the heuristics and biases program. Therefore, by applying it unreflectively to predict firm strategic decisions and outcomes, we may incur the risk of "forfeiting the intellectual challenges thrown off by real-world problems" (Fischhoff, 1996: 246). In Section 5, we will offer some ideas on how to approach and circumvent this fundamental problem. In sum, while Simon's (1947) introduction of the notion of bounded rationality set in motion what may well be described as a revolution, that revolution remains quite unfinished, offering significant opportunities for research in the subfield of behavioral strategy.

3 Managerial and Organizational Cognition: Interpretive Microfoundations of Strategy

Introduction

In recent years, the strategy field dramatically increased its exploration of the cognitive dimensions underlying firms' strategic decisions (e.g., Hodgkinson, 1997; Walsh, 1995). This movement was driven by a recognition that managerial cognition plays an instrumental role in shaping strategic outcomes, fostering innovation, and ensuring organizational adaptability in increasingly volatile and complex environments. This section provides an overview of the historical development of theory and research applying cognitive psychology and social cognition to the analysis of behavior in organizations. Although it originated with Simon's (1947) notion of bounded rationality, this research tradition took a very different path, relying on Weick's (1979) idea of enacted sensemaking and individuals' subjective differences in perception. The section covers three important theoretical perspectives in this stream: (1) schema theory and the related construct of mental maps/representations, (2) social identity theory and self-categorization, and (3) enactment and sensemaking, along with the related view of organizations as interpretative systems. Finally, it discusses some theoretical and empirical challenges in moving forward in the study of these topics. Overall, the section offers an overview of the microfoundational work examining how managers actively perceive, interpret, constitute, and act upon their business environments, and in turn, how these cognitive processes affect firm behavior and outcomes.

Simon's Bounded Rationality Challenged: Weick's Interpretative Perspective

As discussed in Chapter 2, Simon's (1947) notion of bounded rationality is foundational in understanding human decision-making in organizations. At its core, bounded rationality posits that decision-makers are unable to make perfectly rational decisions due to cognitive limitations and the complexity of real-world situations. They thus strive for rationality within the boundaries of their cognitive capacities and information availability (March & Simon, 1958). This realist perspective considers the environment as an external entity, independent of individuals' perceptions or beliefs, and views knowledge as something that is discovered, measured, and generalized. As a result, the focus of this perspective is to arrive at, as much as possible, an objective understanding of the world in the face of uncertainty.

Yet, in the late 1970s and early 1980s, Karl Weick challenges this goal of an objective understanding of reality in Simon's bounded rationality through his work on enactment and the related notion of sensemaking. He argues that sensemaking, a continuous process through which individuals develop meanings based on local actions and experiences, gives rise to a variety of subjective – and potentially divergent – perceptions of the business environment (Weick, 1979). Thus, instead of viewing the world as a homogenous reality to be uncovered, Weick espouses a constructivist approach, viewing the environment as continuously formulated and reformulated through social interactions and interpretations.

Influenced by Weick's work as well as by a burgeoning interest in cognition in the field of social psychology (cf. Fiske & Taylor, 1984), management scholars in the early 1980s began to embrace the view of the environment as socially constructed (e.g., Bartunek, 1984; Daft & Weick, 1984; Huff, 1982; Spender, 1989; Walsh & Fahey, 1986). As a result, researchers examine how managers use cognitive frames to make sense of the environment, and how this sensemaking shapes their strategic choices and actions (Daft & Weick, 1984; Kaplan, 2011).

Naturally, this move toward a socially constructed view translates into significant methodological shifts. Aligning with its objectivist worldview, research building on Simon's notion of bounded rationality predominantly deploys computational models and quantitative tools, intending to reveal and quantify overarching cognitive patterns (e.g., Simon & Newell, 1976). In contrast, the emerging interpretive trend utilizes qualitative methodologies, such as cognitive mapping techniques (e.g., repertory grid technique), ethnographic studies, in-depth interviews, and narrative inquiries. Unlike models or quantitative approaches, these qualitative approaches allow for the exploration of multifaceted cognitive processes, the dynamism of sensemaking, and the contextually embedded construction of knowledge (e.g., Bougon, Weick, & Binkhorst, 1977).

Yet, the study of such cognitive processes continues to pose substantial theoretical and methodological challenges due to fragmentation, construct proliferation, aggregation issues, and validity concerns.

Theoretical Perspectives on Managerial and Organizational Cognition

Three major perspectives pervade existing interpretative work on cognition in organizations: (1) schema theory including mental maps/representations (e.g., strategic groups and framing), (2) social identity theory and self-categorization, and (3) sensemaking and the related view of organizations as interpretative systems.

Schema Theory, Mental Representations, and Frames

Schemas are cognitive structures through which individuals recognize, process, organize, and interpret information from their environment. Rooted in cognitive psychology, schema theory posits these mental frameworks guide humans' perceptions, beliefs, and actions by providing a structured means of understanding. In essence, schemas are the "mental templates" that individuals use to categorize the world (Walsh, 1995).

When applying this theory, strategy scholars tend to assume information converges and is interpreted at the top manager level (Fahey & Narayanan, 1989; Lyles & Schwenk, 1992). Thus, researchers examine how managers' schemas influence their interpretations of complex business environments, their expectations of how these may evolve (Gick & Holyoak, 1983), and their subsequent strategic decisions (Kaplan, 2011). To do so, these scholars generate managers' mental maps or representations, which are "tangible" expressions of schemas, by outlining managerial perceptions and beliefs of the internal and external environment of the firm. These mental maps may include firm structure, technology, industry landscapes, stakeholder interplay, and competitive dynamics

(Kaplan, 2011). For instance, prominent work by Huff (1982), Porac et al. (1989), and Reger and Huff (1993) shed light on the role mental maps play in shaping managerial perceptions of strategic groupings and competitive positioning. While some of these studies indicate strategists within a given sector tend to hold highly similar representations of the competitive landscape (e.g., Porac et al., 1989; Reger & Huff, 1993), others suggest these representations reflect subjective perceptions (Rindova & Fomburn, 1999), prompting radically different strategic groupings across firms in the same industry (e.g., Hodgkinson & Johnson, 1994) within the same timeframe (e.g., Fahey & Narayanan, 1989). One such example is from Kilduff (2019), in which he argues that managers may interpret certain firms as relational rivals (similar to long-standing university rivals), increasing the likelihood of nonrational competitive actions and reactions, exceeding those predicted from market conditions.

Closely related to schema theory is *framing theory* (Goffman, 1974), where frames define the way experience is organized, described, and presented (Cornelissen & Wener, 2014; Fiss & Zajac, 2004; Hodgkinson et al., 1999). By influencing the categorization process (Starbuck & Milliken, 1988), frames determine the perceived importance, urgency, or relevance that managers attribute to issues and events (Jackson & Dutton, 1988), activate expectations about potential outcomes (Goffman, 1974), shape how attention is allocated (Benner & Tripsas, 2012; Ocasio & Joseph, 2005), and influence how strategy is formulated (Dutton, Fahey, & Narayanan, 1983; Kaplan, 2008) and implemented (Thomas, Clark, & Gioia, 1993).

One prolific stream of this strategy research examines how frames impact decision-makers' categorizations and responses to stakeholder evaluations (Bitektine, 2011; Elsbach, 2003). For example, some studies show that the way decision-makers frame stakeholders' feedback results in more or less symbolic responses (e.g., Bass et al., 2023; Nason, Bacq, & Gras, 2018; Wang et al., 2022). In contrast, another stream highlights how mental representations and frames, despite their advantages for information processing and meaning construction, lead to rigidities (Benner & Tripsas, 2012; Gilbert, 2006; Lovallo, Clarke, & Camerer, 2012) that can, in turn, introduce biases or blind spots in the strategic decision-making process (e.g., Barr et al., 1992; Tripsas & Gavetti, 2000). This work suggests that socialization with other relevant actors, including social class peers, business advisors, and family members may alter preexisting schemas, potentially reducing this negative effect (Bartunek & Moch, 1987; Nason, Mazzelli, & Carney, 2019; Strike & Rerup, 2016).

The conceptual apparatus provided by schema and framing theories is cross-level, and microfoundational, offering individual-level explanations for higher-level organizational phenomena. Nevertheless, the field faces challenges due to the proliferation and inconsistent application of related constructs. This issue is particularly evident in the overlapping and sometimes interchangeable use of terms such as mental representations, cognitive frames, frameworks, schemas, maps, and knowledge structures (Walsh, 1995). For behavioral strategy research to progress, it is crucial to achieve greater conceptual clarity. This entails precisely defining each construct and delineating their specific roles and interactions in the context of interpretation and strategic decision-making. Furthermore, despite notable attempts (e.g., Kaplan, 2008), further empirical evidence is needed to examine the mechanisms through which individual-level cognitions translate into collective cognition or shared mental models, especially in the presence of spatial and temporal distances between organizational members.

Social Identity Theory, Self-Categorization, and Organizational Identification

Social psychology theories based on identity and self-categorization suggest individuals delineate groups based on perceived features and then affiliate themselves with those satisfying their personal needs for self-definition and meaning (Tajfel, 1978; Hogg & Terry, 2000; Tajfel & Turner, 1986). This social categorization process shapes member behaviors. That is, individuals incorporate distinctive group features into their own identity (Tajfel & Turner, 1986; Terry & Hogg, 1996) and embrace a shared set of values and beliefs, fostering ingroup cohesion and normative behavior (Brewer & Gardner, 1996; Tajfel & Turner, 1986). Moreover, this delineation is preserved, as ingroup members craft their attributes, norms, and values relative to outgroups to achieve "optimal distinctiveness" (Brewer, 1991).

Ashforth and Mael's (1989) work illuminates the role of organizations (and their subgroups) in organizational members' social identity construction and its impact on the firm (see Ashforth, Harrison, & Corley, 2008; Ashforth & Johnson, 2001; Dutton, Dukerich, & Harquail, 1994; Liu, Fisher, & Chen, 2018).[4] For instance, some scholars illustrate how CEO organizational identification – defined as a CEO's sense of oneness or belongingness with an organization (Lange, Boivie, & Westphal, 2015; Mael & Ashforth, 1992) – can foster goal alignment (Davis, Schoorman, & Donaldson, 1997; Kogut & Zander, 1996), reducing agency costs and, in turn, increasing firm performance (Boivie et al., 2011). Relatedly, other scholarly work examines how a CEO's

---

[4] Because research on organizational identity (e.g., Albert & Whetten, 1985; for a review see Gioia et al., 2013) anthropomorphizes the firm and applies psychological theories directly to the organizational level of analysis, it cannot be considered microfoundational. As such, it falls outside of the boundaries of behavioral strategy according to the definition provided in Section 1.

identification within a particular group in the organization, or adoption of a specific role, shapes their priorities and conduct (e.g., Miller & Breton-Miller, 2011; Miller, Breton-Miller, & Lester, 2011).

This work on social identity branches out beyond CEOs. Literature on group faultlines – referred to as virtual dividing lines that split a group into relatively homogeneous subgroups based on group members' alignment and identification with the subgroup prototype (Lau & Murnighan, 1998; Thatcher & Patel, 2012) investigates how organizational members' multiple identities and their relationships shape firm strategy and performance (Lawrence & Zyphur, 2011). For example, Leicht-Deobalda et al. (2021) show that organizational identification among firm employees can be hampered by demographic faultlines, especially when functional heterogeneity within demographic subgroups is low, in turn, generating negative consequences for firm performance and innovation. Kaczmarek, Kimino, and Pye (2012) article illustrates how task-related faultlines within corporate boards can have value-destroying effects. Faultlines also have a similar effect in top management teams. Although TMT heterogeneity positively impacts the formulation of deviant competitive actions (Ndofor, Sirmon, & He, 2015), this benefit disappears when strong faultlines are present. This represents a more nuanced view of the impact of demographic characteristics on firm performance in the upper echelon's research stream (Hambrick & Mason, 1984).

Despite these important contributions, the literature on how social identification impacts firm behavior and outcomes is still in its infancy, especially when examining the dark side of overidentification in organizations (Bouchikhi & Kimberly, 2003; Fiol, 1991, 2001). Furthermore, significant empirical challenges exist in reliably assessing whether and to what extent social identification affects distal firm-level variables (cf. Ashforth et al., 2008).

Enactment and Sensemaking

As mentioned, Weick's (1979) pioneering work on enactment and sensemaking is at the heart of the interpretative perspectives on managerial cognition. These intertwined constructs assume managers actively shape, or "enact," their environments through their interpretations and actions, rather than passively receiving environmental stimuli (Sutcliffe, 2013; see Maitlis & Sonenshein, 2010 for a review). Weick (1995) elucidates seven properties of sensemaking: (1) identity construction, (2) retrospective analysis, (3) enactive, (4) social, (5) ongoing, (6) focused on extracted cues, and (7) driven by plausibility rather than accuracy. These properties underscore the subjective and often post hoc nature of interpretation, emphasizing that sensemaking is not about uncovering objective truths but rather constructing plausible narratives (Balogun & Johnson, 2005).

The stream of work on enactment and sensemaking highlights how organizational members socially construct their environments by developing shared meanings to rationalize ambiguous events and situations (Elsbach, Barr, & Hargadon, 2005; Ford & Baucus, 1987; Perrow, 1984 Weick, 1988, 2010). For instance, sensemaking is triggered in contexts where expectations are violated (Daft & Weick, 1984), such as during environmental jolts and organizational crises (e.g., Christianson et al., 2009; Meyer, 1982) as well as in response to identity threats (e.g., Elsbach & Kramer, 1996; Ravasi & Schulz, 2006; Weick, 1995). According to this perspective, action and discourse are the main means to create understanding, allowing organizational members to "consolidate an otherwise unorganized set of environmental elements" and achieve intersubjective meaning creation (Weick, 1988: 135).

Top managers and other influential organizational members have an important role in guiding collective sensemaking processes (Balogun & Johnson, 2004; Monin et al., 2013). To capture this notion, Gioia and Chittipeddi (1991) introduced the concept of sensegiving, where influential figures within organizations attempt to shape the perceptions of others, promoting certain understandings of events and situations. This work emphasizes the leaders' roles in crafting and framing organizational narratives as "the preferred sensemaking currency" (Boje, 1991: 161; e.g., Brown, Stacey, & Nandhakumar, 2008; Maitlis & Lawrence, 2007).

Likely the most significant way in which sensemaking research influences strategy research is through work elucidating how sensemaking enables or inhibits key organizational processes, including learning (Christianson et al., 2009; Thomas, Sussman, & Henderson, 2001), strategic change (Corley & Gioia, 2004; Nag et al., 2007), and innovation (Dougherty et al., 2000; Jay, 2013). A clear theme emerging from this literature is the importance of sensemaking in developing novel meanings that underpin new ways of understanding and organizing.

As the business landscape grows in complexity and uncertainty, Weick's interpretative lens becomes increasingly salient. Future endeavors should build on his rich theoretical bedrock by comparing multiple instances of sensemaking to examine when and how individuals collectively construct new meanings and how this process affects firm behavior and outcomes. Because sensemaking intersects with other theoretical domains, there is also a need to clarify the boundaries of this construct to ensure its theoretical distinctiveness.

Conclusion: The Future of Managerial and Organizational Cognition

Frames and mental representations, social identity and identification, and sensemaking emerge as important constructs to elucidate the microfoundations of firm behavior and outcomes. For example, when industry environments change, schema theory and the related concepts of frames and mental representations point to the cognitive frameworks that strategists use to recognize, interpret, and negotiate unfamiliar information from the external environment, enabling managers to classify information and form subjective representations of the environment, including social evaluations. Similarly, the constructs of social identity and identification shed light on how managers' personal and social self-concepts influence the impact of organizational design on firm strategic choices. Finally, sensemaking anchors schemas and identity in the realm of dynamic interpretation and meaning-making. It emphasizes the ongoing nature of understanding, suggesting that strategists continually weave and reweave their narratives to retrospectively make and give sense to what occurs. This is also particularly important for understanding microfoundations of competitive advantage. As the external environment changes, managers with different views of their organizations are likely to develop divergent interpretations, suggesting that responses to environmental changes may be different.

Looking ahead, behavioral strategy researchers interested in the role of cognition in organizations will need to confront challenges concerning theoretical fragmentation and construct proliferation, the need for empirical evidence of aggregation mechanisms, and validity. In particular, despite the fundamental synergies between the various perspectives presented, we are still a long way from a truly integrated interpretative perspective. The main hurdles come from the proliferation and inconsistent use of constructs. First, there is a significant ontological divide on whether cognition is solely an individual-level construct or if a collective supra-individual cognition also exists (Maitlis & Sonenshein, 2010; Walsh, 1995). Relatedly, some scholars view sensemaking as a within-individual process through which one develops schema and mental models (e.g., Hill & Levenhagen, 1995; Starbuck & Milliken, 1988), whereas others conceive it as inherently social (e.g., Maitlis, 2005; Weick, 2005). This tension could probably be resolved by providing evidence of the mechanisms through which organizational members "produce, negotiate, and sustain a shared sense of meaning" (Gephart et al., 2010: 285). Being explicit in the level of analysis and producing empirical evidence of cross-level mechanisms would also be important to avoid arbitrary anthropomorphizing tendencies (granting organizations analogous agency to think and act as humans (cf. Whetten, 2006: 221)), which may undermine the importance of strategy microfoundations.

Still, such mechanisms are extremely difficult to observe, measure, and compare, as they are highly contextual. Even though scholars have established and employed an impressive array of procedures to produce fine-grained empirical accounts – including case studies, ethnographies, text analysis, and cognitive mapping techniques – doubts remain regarding the adequacy of these techniques and their relative merits (Hodgkinson & Healey, 2008). We see value in methods that allow for systematic comparisons, such as causal mapping, as it may allow future research to shed light on relevant contextual contingencies and, thus, specify boundary conditions on existing theory. We will return to some of these methods in Section 5.

4 Behavioral Governance: Synthesizing Carnegie-Based and Governance Perspectives

Introduction

Research on governance – the mechanisms deployed to control or coordinate organizational agents or exchanges within or between firms (alternative contracts and governance structures) – developed independent of the various behavioral strategy theories. Governance research traditionally arose from the organizational economics literature (e.g., Jensen & Meckling, 1976; Williamson, 1985), which did not overlap with the behavioral strategy literatures. However, when governance research is augmented with psychology, a place for governance theories emerged in behavioral strategy. Thus, adding realistic behavioral assumptions to traditional governance theories (e.g., agency theory and TCE) allows us to bring this work together with organizational design research (e.g., Galbraith, 1973; Burton & Obel, 2018) and the attention-based view of the firm (Ocasio, 1997) in a novel research agenda that we term *behavioral governance*.

We envision behavioral governance as an approach that draws on realistic behavioral assumptions to design systems, mechanisms, or organizations to promote coordination and cooperation between parties. This approach considers information salience, flow, and interpretation, in addition to the mitigation of agency or transaction costs arising from cognitive and emotional sources. It leads to two main objectives of this section. The first goal is to highlight the importance of aligning the behavioral assumptions in traditional governance theories with those in the attention-based view and organizational design literatures. This is a necessary step to allow the three literatures to be used together and to build on one another. The second goal is to then bring these three areas of research together to create an exciting research stream that offers managers, with limited attention and information as well as a myriad of motivations, realistic guidance for designing governance with minimal transaction costs arising from conflict and coordination issues between the parties.

To understand the promise of behavioral governance, we start by briefly sketching the Carnegie tradition (Simon, 1947; March & Simon, 1958) and its links to these three literatures (economic governance augmented with psychology, organizational design, and the attention-based view of the firm) to understand why bringing them together augments our understanding of governance design. Then we present the attention-based view of the firm and organizational design literatures, noting their realistic behavioral assumptions. Next, we explore the nascent work on augmenting economic-based theories of the firm. Finally, we examine how bringing these three perspectives together creates significant opportunities for future research in behavioral governance.

Behavioral Roots in the Carnegie Tradition

As discussed in Sections 2 and 3, the Carnegie tradition concentrated on decision-making in the organization based on realistic behavioral assumptions, and how this leads to firm-level actions such as resource allocation. This multidisciplinary approach was a reaction to the firm-level focus of economic theory at the time. Simon (1948) introduced the idea of bounded rationality, suggesting that "human behavior is intendedly rational but only limitedly so" due to cognitive constraints. Large swaths of organization theory were directly based on this idea, and of course, March and Simon's (1958) *Organizations*, another foundational work in the Carnegie school, further extended bounded rationality in an organizational context. Specifically, it examined how bounded rationality leads to "simplified subjective representations of objective reality" (Bromiley et al., 2019: 1519) in organizations, influencing all managerial decision-making. They also argued that organizations are mechanisms for coordinating information flows to increase exchange performance. Together, these aspects are the basis of the information-processing perspective, in which the organizational design literature and the attention-based view are rooted.

Finally, Cyert and March's (1963: 19) *Behavioral Theory of the Firm* used these concepts to examine "the fundamental decisions of the firm, decisions such as price, output, and resource allocation." As a result, they predicted how "a firm behaves as a result of lower-level processes, possibly involving individual and group, and certainly leading to observable decisions on economically important variables" (Gavetti, Greve, Levinthal, & Ocasio, 2012: 3). This book specifically brought in the idea of power and politics, and how to design the organization to mitigate these issues, which again is similar to the psychologically augmented economic-based governance research.

Yet, despite the common roots in the Carnegie tradition, economic-based governance theory is not typically combined with organizational design research or the attention-based view because the underlying behavioral assumptions are incompatible. That is, while the attention-based view and the organizational design literatures embrace a full spectrum of motivations and bounds on individuals' rationality, the economic-based governance literature does not.

Behavioral Governance Theories with Realistic Behavioral Assumptions

As suggested, both the attention-based view of the firm (Ocasio, 1997) and the organizational design literature (e.g., Galbraith, 1973; Burton & Obel, 2018) fully embrace individuals' cognitive limits and motivations. The attention-based view explores how the firm directs management and employee attention, influencing firm behavior. Furthermore, the field of organizational design examines how the arrangement of organizational units and authority impacts knowledge flows.

The Attention-Based View of the Firm

Ocasio (1997) expanded Simon's (1961) bounded rationality into the attention-based view of the firm, which addresses coordination inside the firm. He specifically suggested that firm behavior results from the way in which firms direct the attention of the individuals within it. As such, the organizational actors' information is both limited and distorted by the firm in which they work. This approach is frequently used in both theoretical work (Ocasio & Joseph, 2005) and empirical studies (e.g., Bouquet & Birkinshaw, 2008; Bouquet, et al., 2009; Hung, 2005; Ocasio & Joseph, 2008). For example, Joseph and Wilson (2018) used the attention-based view to predict when the firm will expand to include new subunits to address intrafirm attentional conflicts. This type of work explores using organizational design to direct employee attention to increase coordination.

Organization Design

There is also a large body of work on organization design (e.g., Galbraith 1973; Burton & Obel, 2018). This research stream addresses coordination and cooperation inside the firm. That is, organizational design research "investigate[s] the information flows essential for accomplishing the organization's objectives, then examine[s] what these information patterns imply for organization structure" (Simon, 1967: 1). This work relies on the simplistic mental representations proposed by March and Simon (1958), and the influence that organizational structure has on them. Thus, organizational actors in this theory have both limits on the amount of information processed, as well as distortions of this information due to the organization's design. There are many studies in this area that examine how these information processing needs lead to centralization and decentralization in the organization (e.g., Obel & Burton, 1984; Galbraith, 1973, 1977; Thompson, 1967; Tushman & Nadler, 1978).

Augmenting Economic-Based Governance Theory with Psychology

In contrast to the focus on information flows and attention, economic-based governance theories focus on the design of effective exchanges within and between firms to mitigate transaction costs. Two main theories guide this study: agency theory and TCE.

Agency theory examines how a principal delegates a task to a self-interested agent (Jensen & Meckling, 1976). The principal, the residual claimant, pays the agent for their work. However, because their interests differ, the agent is not likely to act in the interest of the principal without proper incentives (Eisenhardt, 1989). Specifically, this approach focuses on designing the optimal contract to align principal and agent interests.

Transaction cost economics (Williamson, 1985) focuses instead on minimizing transaction costs in the exchange by discriminately aligning ex post governance structure with transaction hazards (Williamson, 1975; 1985). In this theory, boundedly rational actors create unavoidably incomplete contracts, which cannot safeguard an exchange characterized by asset specificity, the presence of highly specific assets with no value in another exchange (Riordan & Williamson, 1985). Asset specificity allows one party to holdup the other, creating transaction costs in the exchange. That is, an opportunistic party can take advantage of the party with the specific investment because the latter has no other options. As such, transaction hazards pose a significant risk for parties in an exchange, as ex post adaptation is likely, and cannot be fully safeguarded against in a contract. Williamson (1991) then discriminately matches the level of the transaction hazard with three governance forms (market, hybrids, and hierarchy) based on their ability to mitigate them. In his analysis, markets efficiently govern transactions with low asset specificity, while hierarchies efficiently govern those with high specificity, and hybrids best govern those in between.

Misaligned Behavioral Assumptions

However, the behavioral assumptions underlying these two economic-based theories do not match those of the attention-based view and organization design, making it difficult to combine them. In particular, agency theory is firmly based on the traditional economics model of maximization. Transaction cost economics, which creates a discriminating alignment between exchange characteristics and efficient governance to mitigate transaction costs, assumes boundedly rational actors. Even with these assumptions, the theories narrowly define actors' cognitive limitations, in the case of TCE including bounds on the amount of information they process (Foss & Weber, 2016) and in the case of principal-agent theory recognizing no such bounds but postulating asymmetric information conditions. The thin bounded rationality assumption of TCE (Foss, 2001) allows all contracts to be unavoidably incomplete, which is necessary for agency and transaction costs to arise ex post (Eisenhardt, 1989; Williamson, 1985). However, it ignores the distortions due to cognitive biases and heuristics (e.g., Tversky and Kahneman, 1974) that Simon intended. Thus, as conceived, it is incompatible with the full form of bounded rationality assumed in both the organizational design and the attention-based view literatures.

Moreover, both theories focus solely on negative motivations. Agency theory only considers self-interest, suggesting agents act in their own interest, unless these are aligned with those of the agent (Eisenhardt, 1989). TCE takes this self-interested view further by assuming an even stronger form of self-interest, opportunism. Opportunism is self-interest seeking "with guile" (Williamson, 1985), which permits actors to lie, cheat, and steal in pursuit of their own interests, as they are not constrained by laws and rules. Again, the motivational assumptions of these economic-based governance theories are incompatible with those of organizational design research and the attention-based view, which both allow for more expansive positive (e.g., reciprocity) or negative (e.g., internal politics) motivations.

Given these extensive differences in both cognitive and motivational assumptions of economic-based governance theories and the attention-based view and organizational design literatures, there is a need to augment the less complex behavioral assumptions of the former to bring them in line with those of the latter. Some work has started to do just that. However, this work has only begun to scratch the surface of expanding these behavioral assumptions for governance.

Behavioral Agency Theory

Scholars expanded the behavioral assumptions of agency theory in two ways. First, they put bounded rationality assumptions in the form of cognitive distortions explicitly into the foundations of the theory. Second, they increased the precision of negative motivations, as well as added positive motivations into agency theory.

Cognitive Expansion. Behavioral agency theory augments agency theory with a variety of cognitive constraints that distort the information processes. Specifically, problem framing, drawing on prospect theory (Kahneman & Tversky, 1979), was added to address agent risk-taking behavior (Wiseman & Gomez-Mejia, 1998), with greater risk-taking linked to positive versus negative framing. Further, Foss and Stea (2014) augmented agency theory with boundedly rational sensemaking, allowing the principal to learn the agent's effort and type. This addition allowed for the reduction of information asymmetry, leading to greater value creation in the exchange than predicted by traditional agency theory.

Motivational Expansion. More recent work elaborated on the motivational assumptions of agency theory. The broad concept of self-interest was replaced with the negative emotions of envy, guilt, and greed, and augmented with the positive motivation of fairness (Pepper, Gosling, & Gore, 2015). This greater specificity was better able to explain the results found in empirical data than the rational choice model. Further, Bosse and Phillips (2016) combined traditional agency theory with the positive motivations of reciprocity and fairness to limit self-interest, resulting in the expansion of the theory from simply limiting self-serving agent behaviors to expanding social welfare. Further, Pepper and Gore (2015) centered the agents in the theory, suggesting motivated managers tended to perform better than those with incentives aligned with the principal. Finally, Cuevas-Rodríguez, Gomez-Mejia, and Wiseman (2012) added trust to suggest that agents can behave honestly and loyally, leading to cooperative relationships with the principal.

Behavioral Transaction Cost Economics

Additionally, since the inception of TCE, scholars continued to offer expansions of the behavioral assumptions underlying the theory (e.g., Ouchi, 1980; Ghoshal & Moran, 1996). As with behavioral agency theory, this augmentation resulted in different predictions than traditional TCE.

Cognitive Expansion. Like agency theory, TCE's bounded rationality assumption was also expanded. In the context of contractual governance, Weber and Mayer (2011) examined how contract frames impact views of the exchange, emotions, behaviors, and exchange relationships. Further, Weber and Bauman (2019) empirically extended this theory by uncovering attributions of benevolence as the underlying psychological mechanism. Additional research in this area examined how regulatory focus impacts contract design (Weber, Mayer, & Macher, 2011), as well as how contract design influences trust development and learning in repeated exchanges (Weber 2017), and innovation (Mayer, Xing, & Mondal, 2022). Finally, Weber and Coff (2023) elaborated on the idea of cognitive biases to suggest asset specificity perceptions drive most governance decisions, and these perceptions are likely to be biased and even manipulated.

Foss and Weber (2016) moved the discussion of augmented bounded rationality away from contract framing. Instead, they focused on how bounded rationality alone may lead to specific transaction costs inside the firm. Moreover, Nickerson and co-authors drew on an expanded bounded rationality assumption to identify antecedents to governance decisions, creating the problem formulation-problem solving perspectives (e.g., Nickerson, Silverman, & Zenger, 2007; Baer, Dirks, & Nickerson, 2009).

Motivational Expansion. Additionally, due to the concern over Williamson's negative motivational assumption in TCE (Ghoshal & Moran, 1996), scholars expanded this behavioral assumption. Ouchi (1980) brought social comparison into TCE, introducing clan governance to address it. Moreover, Ouchi and Barney (1980) suggested goal alignment influences the efficient governance form, expanding the options from market and hierarchy to include clans, bureaucracies, quasi-markets, and their intermediate forms. Further, Husted and Folger (2004) elaborated on this idea, incorporating organizational justice into the theory and arguing that transaction costs typically occur because it is difficult to assess fairness in an exchange. Nickerson and Zenger (2008) further expanded on the incorporation of social comparison in TCE, showing that these comparisons and their resulting negative emotions can lead to hierarchical failure, as they and their associated costs increase with the scope and scale of the firm. More recently, Weber, Foss, and Lindenberg (2023) expanded Williamson's opportunism assumption into different types of opportunisms, as well as added the positive motivation of cooperation. Specifically, they suggested that different hierarchical forms tend to invoke distinct motivations, which lead to specific behaviors.

A Behavioral Governance Research Agenda

Simon (1985: 303) argued that in thinking about designing a transaction for optimal performance, "[n]othing is more fundamental in setting our research agenda and informing our research methods than our view of the nature of the human beings whose behavior we are studying." By augmenting economic-based governance theory with psychology, we contend it can be combined with the

attention-based view and organizational design to create high-performance transactions within and between firms. This goal suggests two separate but critical
future research streams in behavioral governance to gain a more realistic understanding of how to design efficient transactions.

Psychology-Augmented Governance Theory

First, the work on augmenting economic-based governance theories with psychology is in its infancy. While work on contract framing has gained some traction,
there are still ample opportunities to examine the impact of other bounds on
rationality in these theories. Moreover, the studies on expanding motivations and
adding the impact of external environments on governance are just starting to
emerge. Finally, the idea of bringing in informational, attentional, and governance
issues together to design high-performance transactions has not yet been done.
Thus, this area of research is wide-open, offering extensive opportunities for future
work.

Opportunities to Expand Bounded Rationality. There are several areas for
additional research in expanding the bounded rationality assumption in
economic-based governance theories. First, behavioral agency theory is much
less developed than behavioral TCE. As a result, research on the impact of
framing tasks and incentives, beyond those using prospect theory (Kahneman
& Tversky, 1979), should be considered, as the prior work using prospect theory
has been criticized as improperly applying base predictions from the lens to
the firm (Bromiley, 2010). For example, considering the impact of prevention
and promotion framing in agency theory could create interesting prescriptions
for managers who are looking to induce vigilant versus eager behavior in their
agents.

Additionally, even in TCE, the work on framing only considered regulatory
focus theory. However, there are other ways to frame the same contract. For
example, the contract's time horizon could be framed as short term versus long
term. Additionally, contract detail could be framed at a high-level or extremely
detailed, based on construal theory. Moreover, the exchange relationship
between the partners can be framed as competitive or cooperative. Thus, there
are many different possibilities for framing the exact same contract that have not
yet been explored.

Another distortion of human cognition emerges from stereotypes. While
organizational behavior research examines how gender and racial stereotypes
impact individual career paths and job satisfaction, this work does not examine
how these cognitive elements influence transactions within and between firms.
Yet, these stereotypes can influence organizational actors' perceptions of

opportunistic behavior or the attributions of benevolence, directly impacting transaction performance. Further, while some studies explore attributions of performance in exchanges, no one explicitly examines when the fundamental attribution error may occur, which may impact the formation of trust, as well as the perception of opportunistic behavior in the exchange. As such, both aspects of governance are virtually unexplored at this time.

In addition, only one study (Weber & Coff, 2023) examines the biases and malleability of perceptions of key TCE constructs, such as asset specificity, uncertainty, and frequency. Additionally, the concept of perceptions has not been brought into agency theory at all. Yet, in both cases, it is likely that perceptions of these key constructs drive both choices and behaviors in these theories. Thus, it is imperative to understand how incorporating perceptions into these economic-based governance theories may change their predictions and may explain empirical evidence that traditional theories cannot address.

Finally, most psychological theories address individual behaviors, which is appropriate for its application to agency theory. However, TCE discusses firm-level outcomes. Thus, when augmenting TCE with psychology, there is a need to either work with transactions involving a small group of managers or to examine how these effects aggregate to the firm level. That is, the cognitive impact on a single person does not matter unless that impact is likely to dominate the individuals in the transaction. Thus, there is a need for a deeper examination of this topic.

Opportunities to Expand Motivations. In addition to these opportunities to extend the cognitive assumptions in agency theory and TCE, there is also a need for research that expands the motivational assumptions of these theories. For example, nonconscious affect could impact contract design. That is, witnessing a supplier manager berating their assistant during a negotiation, may unconsciously activate negative exchange attitudes, leading to the inclusion of more safeguards in the contract.

Moreover, while emotions are examined as an outcome variable in behavioral governance, their influence on transaction costs or governance is not yet explored. Emotions were shown to impact both cognition and motivation. Thus, they are good candidates for future exploration in economic-based governance theories.

Additionally, most motivations examined in agency theory and TCE are broad. That is, self-interest and opportunism are both negative, but not precise motivations. Thus, there is also a need to expand the types of opportunisms that may be motivating specific behaviors. So far, only one paper explores a more nuanced look at opportunism (Weber, Foss, & Lindenberg, 2023). Further, while a few positive motivations are incorporated into agency theory (e.g., Devers, Cannella, Reilly, & Yoder, 2007), fewer are incorporated into TCE. Thus, there is a broad area of motivational expansion that can occur in economic-based governance theory.

Finally, while the expansion of TCE's motivations started with social comparison, little empirical research examines envy costs. In addition, there has not been an application of this concept to alliances or contracts. As a result, there is a significant opportunity to explore this extension as well.

Holistic Behavioral Governance Theories

There are also several opportunities to bring attention, knowledge flows, and governance together to design optimal transactions within and between firms. For example, incentives can be used to increase knowledge flows. Further, organizational design can impact perceptions of transaction hazards, impacting governance choice. To understand the potential for this combination to expand our understanding of transaction performance, we explore a few of these potential areas of interest in detail.

Situated Cognition and Motivation in Governance. First, there is a chance to bring in the attention-based view of the firm to understand how perceptions of governance variables are formed, and how they may be biased. Additionally, by bringing concepts of organizational design into governance, Williamson's concept of administrative mechanisms can be expanded to include centralization and decentralization, as well as other aspects of structure. Further, organizational structures are likely to impact managers' and employees' motivations, which also can be used to inform contracts in agency theory. As there may be opportunities to shape agent behavior without aligning their incentives in an employment contract.

Design to Optimize Organization Performance. In addition, organizational design may increase or reduce the need for governance, while potentially also allowing for optimal information flow. Thus, rather than focusing on one aspect of the other, the field can return to multi-theoretical perspectives, such as those that dominated economic-based strategy in the early 2000s (transaction cost plus the resource-based view, for example), but in a behavioral strategy realm. Neither information flows nor governance are mutually exclusive in an organization. Instead, each aspect likely influences the other, so it is important to understand how these elements work together or in opposition when designing the organization.

Design to Optimize Transaction Performance. Moreover, the only research examining how transactions are designed is within the context of organizations (i.e., the organizational design literature). While this is an interesting topic, the governance literature is also interested in how transactions between firms (e.g., alliances) or within markets are designed. Given that not all markets, contracts, or alliances are the same, but instead may have many different characteristics, these may be used as design levers to both increase information flows and minimize transaction costs. Also, these different governance forms shape actors' attention, which further impacts their perceptions in these transactions, bringing in the attention-based view (Ocasio, 1997).

Tradeoffs between Informational Benefits and Transaction Costs. Finally, there are likely tradeoffs between optimizing information flow and minimizing transaction costs. There is a huge opportunity to examine when these would occur and the most effective solutions to address them. There is also a significant prospect to examine how to potentially shape managers' or employees' attention to avoid these tradeoffs.

Conclusion

The promise of behavioral governance is significant. By augmenting economic-based governance theory with psychology, we can create common behavioral assumptions, allowing us to bring together attention, design, and governance. This multi-theoretical view of transactions within and between organizations is a powerful lens that provides a more complete view of how to optimize all aspects of a transaction, not just transaction cost mitigation, knowledge flow, or managerial attention. Thus, this approach offers a more holistic understanding of transactions, as well as more realistic advice for managers who are overseeing them.

5 Advancing Behavioral Strategy Research: A Microfoundational Roadmap

Behavioral Strategy Research: The Search for Generalizability, Parsimony, and Accuracy

A basic theme of this Element is that behavioral strategy is a fundamentally micro-foundational approach rooted in robust, evidence-based knowledge of human nature, behavior, and social interaction. Despite the many advances in linking the psychology of organizational actors and firms' behaviors and outcomes, much (perhaps most) work in strategy still treats the organization as an almost "mechanistic" entity governed by rules and processes, and acquiring and developing resources and competencies to fulfill the demands of the external environment. Decision-making, including generating, implementing, and executing strategy, easily gets lost in such an account. Surprisingly, this is also a problem in behavioral strategy.

Throughout this Element, we highlighted how behavioral strategy still needs to overcome multiple microfoundational challenges related to theorizing and testing aggregation mechanisms (i.e., Sections 2 and 3), finding unity within diversity (i.e., Sections 3 and 4), enhancing construct clarity and avoiding their proliferation (i.e., Sections 3 and 4), and integrating methods (i.e., Sections 2 and 3). For instance, we argued that concepts such as bounded rationality (Section 2), mental representations (Section 3), and attention (Sections 2 and 4) have been often unreflectively applied to the organizational level. This runs the risk of granting organizations analogous agency to humans. We also highlighted how the same construct (e.g., bounded rationality) has been defined in very different and ways across different research streams (Section 4), how constructs with overlapping theoretical meanings have been given distinct labels (Section 3), and how less stable psychological constructs, such as affect and emotions, have received less attention because of measurability issues (Section 2).

Arguably, some of these issues are rooted in the historical evolution of the field of behavioral strategy and the goals that Simon set for himself and posterity with his theory of decision-making. As mentioned in Section 2, Simon's original goal was to develop a *generalizable, simple,* and *accurate* theory that would have predicted individual choice across a variety of contexts and problem situations. However, as Thorngate argued, "It is impossible for a theory of social behavior to be simultaneously general, simple or parsimonious, and accurate" (1976: 406).[5] Over the years, the balance tilted in favor either of generalizability and parsimony, or accuracy.

Attempts to develop generalizable and parsimonious theories largely resulted in *desubjectification* tendencies, with behavioral scholars shifting attention from the micro level (individuals and their interactions) to the mechanisms governing and stabilizing exchanges among individuals (or, more precisely, coalitions of individuals). For example, to solve the problem of defining organizational goals, Cyert and March shifted their focus away from the conflicting motivations and preferences of individuals and the bargaining processes underlying coalition formation and goal priorities, towards an *assumption* of quasi-resolution of conflict as a mechanism leading to goal stabilization (1963: 30–39) (see Mithani & O'Brien, 2021 for a review). This issue is also pervasive in the upper echelons theory (Hambrick & Mason, 1984): although this theory emphasizes the importance of characterizing the linkages among individuals, organizations, and their competitive environments, it assumes the top management team "embodies" the cognition of the organization.

---

[5] This quote was also used by Weick (1979) in his critique of bounded rationality (Section 3).

On the other hand, attempts to develop realistic and accurate theories have certainly provided rich insights into local meanings and micro practices, but sometimes at the risk of downplaying the connections between local subjective worlds and macro-organizational processes and phenomena (cf. Prasad & Prasad, 2002). Research opportunities may likely emerge from better balancing generalizability and accuracy (at the expense of parsimony). This would require a commitment towards social *contextualization* (i.e., who, what, where, when, why, and how) by adding detail and contextual reality to develop theories with substantially greater power to predict real-world organizational behaviors and outcomes both within and across contexts. In this respect, the first fundamental step is characterizing the organizational member(s) involved in the firm-level phenomenon (or decision) being investigated. It also requires a shift from treating levels of analysis as compartmentalized theoretical domains toward a focus on situated social interactions among relevant actors within and outside the organizations as the loci of aggregation. This new approach may not only overcome some of the aforementioned challenges and fill some of the voids in the current behavioral strategy landscape but also influence the direction of strategy research at large.

More generally, *microfoundations are theoretically generative*: new or revised assumptions about the cognition, motivations, and abilities of individuals and how they interact are likely to result in new theory (Foss & Hallberg, 2014). For example, in Section 4, we argued that bringing in psychological and motivational factors such as contract framing and emotions, may affect governance theories' predictions regarding contractual design and outcomes. In this section, we present a roadmap for future microfoundational research on behavioral strategy, proposing a series of research questions inspired by fundamental considerations about better contextualizing current theories. See the following Table 1.

Theoretical Avenues

The Who?

Most work in behavioral strategy focuses on top managers' decision-making, whereas applications to decision-making at lower levels are less common. However, decision-making at lower levels may impact the phenomena that behavioral strategy researchers are investigating, notably because such decisions may aggregate to firm-level outcomes (e.g., Foss & Weber). Such aggregation may happen through social interaction. Relatedly, a nascent microfoundational stream in strategy research encourages a focus on interfaces – that is, "instances in which individuals' attributes, aspirations, and activities influence one another" – as germane for explicitly considering

Table 1 Behavioral strategy new research areas

Topic	Research Question(s)
Strategic Beliefs and Interfaces	How are strategic beliefs regarding competitive dynamics formed and altered through interfaces within and across organizational boundaries (in the absence of direct communication channels)?
Motivations and Noncognitive Elements	How does intrinsic motivation shape strategic consensus across various organizational groups? What impact do collective emotional events have on the formulation and revision of organizational goals?
Goal Frames and Organizational Performance	How do differences in individual goal frames within cross-functional teams impact the development and execution of organizational strategies?
Imagination and Strategic Narratives	How do shared strategic narratives among employees contribute to generating new solutions under conditions of deficient knowledge and experience?
Predispositions and Unconscious Competence	What mechanisms enable organizations to tap into the collective unconscious competencies to drive innovation?
Coalition Formation Dynamics	What is the role played by emotions, primary needs (e.g., need to belong), as well as stable personality traits, in either counterbalancing or accentuating mental model differences during coalition formation?
Leadership and Mental Models	How do specific goal frames and mental models become dominant, legitimated, and capable of triggering collective action? How does leadership style influence the adoption of different mental models and goal frames in an organization? What is the role of coalition members' characteristics, skills, and personality traits in either facilitating or hindering frame acceptance?

Governance and Mental Model Divergences	What is the effectiveness of different governance forms, agreements, and routines in mitigating deep-level *vs.* surface-level mental model divergences?
	How does organizational structure drive heuristics and biases or particular goal frames, which may augment or hinder cooperation and coordination?
Strategists' Psychology and Organizational Design	How do managers' cognitions, emotions, and motivations impact perceptions of key resources, need for governance, or interest alignment?
	How does cognitive and affective information processing translate into deliberate action aimed at creating new routines and reconfiguring organizational resources and competencies?
Decision-Making and Performance Outcomes	How do characteristics of employees (non-TMT) impact decision-making, especially when organizations require adaptation?
	To what extent do the cognitive, motivational, and affective aspects of social interaction among organizational members explain the relationship between strategic choice and performance outcomes (competitive advantage)?
AI's Role in Decision-Making	What is the impact of AI on the balance between intuition and analysis in strategic decision-making?
	How and to what extent can AI mitigate versus exacerbate cognitive biases?
	What are the advantages and disadvantages of having AI systems mediate sensemaking and social influence processes?
Uncertainty and Adaptive Heuristics	How do organizations develop and modify heuristics to navigate strategic decision-making under radical uncertainty?
	How do organizations develop narratives of a non-yet-existent future?
	What role does sensemaking play in the evolution of heuristics for managing uncertainty?

"both sides of the ledger" in terms of the actors involved" and their proximate and distal organization-level outcomes (Simsek, Heavey, & Fox, 2018: 284). Indeed, interfaces are not only the primary means for strategic leaders to carry out their daily work but also the main conduit for bottom-up influence. For example, Dutton and Ashford (1993) show how middle managers' issue-selling efforts focus senior managers' attention and shape their understanding of strategic issues. and teams outside of the TMT, but catalyzed by the interactions of managers at different levels. Huy, Corley, and Kraatz (2014) shed light on how the emotions of middle-level managers can play a significant role in fostering or hampering the implementation of strategic changes, thus potentially affecting firm adaptation and performance. Sonenshein (2010) highlights how managers' and employees' narratives about strategic change interact to either facilitate or hinder implementation.

In sum, framing the "who" from an interface perspective is likely to trigger questions about what intersects at the interface (e.g., goals, cognitions, emotions). It also prompts investigation into the type of influence at the interface (motivational, cognitive, behavioral), its direction (up, down, lateral), and its pattern (constraining, enabling) (Simsek et al., 2018). This examination offers opportunities to understand which interactions, among whom, shape firm strategies, influence decision-making processes, and ultimately drive firm performance.

The What?

Our discussion of the behavioral strategy landscape so far suggests that existing perspectives largely explore the cognitive side of bounded rationality (Gigerenzer & Goldstein, 1996). Yet, even this topic has not been fully examined, suggesting that there is still significant potential for research in this area. Moreover, noncognitive elements including motivations, goals, emotions, imagination, and predispositions, have not been incorporated into behavioral strategy research. We examine the potential for incorporating these aspects into behavioral strategy research below.

Strategic Beliefs. In traditional decision-making models, beliefs are estimates of the payoffs associated with the decision alternatives. Some scholars suggest that explicitly integrating them into the existing theories may lead to new firm-level predictions, such as search in response to increasing performance (rather than decreasing, as traditionally posited) (e.g., Keil, Posen, & Workiewicz, 2023). Belief updating is another area for potential work in behavioral strategy research. While research on Bayesian approaches to belief updating (e.g., Cyert & DeGroot, 1974; Daw et al., 2011) could be extended to predict firm behaviors and outcomes, it would not solve the basic problem that Bayesianism cannot address unforeseen events, surprises, and novelty (Ehrig & Foss, 2022). Moreover, as March and Olsen point out, individual beliefs and models of the world are not always tied to experience and objective reality – "individuals, as well as organizations or nations, develop myths, fictions, legends, and illusions." (1975: 154). In particular, *ideologies* often serve as lenses through which information is interpreted, guiding how it is assimilated and beliefs are updated (Semadeni, Chin, & Krause, 2022). This interpretation process can, therefore, lead to belief updating that is less about Bayesian adjustments and more about reinforcing existing frameworks and worldviews (Staw & Ross, 1980). Further exploration into the nuances of belief formation and updating in organizations, especially those not rooted in direct experience, may offer valuable insights for behavioral strategy. Indeed, such an exploration would allow for a more dynamic and comprehensive understanding of experience- vs. non-experience-based belief updating. This distinction may make beliefs more or less likely to change, and therefore, have a greater or lesser influence on strategic decisions and competitive outcomes.

Motivations. Motivational issues in general, and employee motivation in particular, are under-explored research avenues in behavioral strategy (with some exceptions, such as Bridoux, Coeurderoy, & Durand, 2011; Lindenberg & Foss 2011). However, there are many opportunities for linking motivations at various levels in the firm to key strategic issues. The current dominant motivational theory is self-determination theory (Deci & Ryan, 2012: 416) which theorizes a spectrum of motivational drivers. Future behavioral strategy research may explore how this fine-grained theory of motivation can be linked to organizational characteristics, different governance instruments and ways of managing, and different aggregate outcomes (e.g., competitive advantage).

Complementing intrinsic and prosocial motivations is "idealism," that is, the pursuit of lofty, often unbounded goals, unconstrained by conventional notions of practicality. This form of idealism, as Schilling (2018: 338) notes, can lead to the formation of superordinate goals, driving individuals towards higher aspirations. Such an idealistic pursuit within organizational contexts can, for example, lead to employee resilience, a relatively unexplored but potentially important source of sustained competitive advantage.

Goals. Combining motivation and cognition, goal frames are an important construct for understanding the microfoundations of value creation, a key concept in strategy research. The basic notion is that behavior is influenced by higher-level goals that, when salient, steer an individual's motivation and cognition. Goal-framing theory proposes different goal frames that are differentially salient to individuals. These goal frames are linked to specific individual behaviors, and also shape firm behaviors in the aggregate (Foss & Lindenberg, 2013; Lindenberg & Foss, 2011).

New research on goal framing may provide more detail on why, how, and when specific goal frames become dominant at the organizational level, fostering collective commitment toward certain choices or actions. Expanding this line of inquiry could involve further exploring the interactions between goal frames and other organizational elements, such as leadership, organizational design, and culture. In particular, in the formation and reinforcement of goal frames that are beneficial to an organization's performance, the interplay of organizational culture, leadership styles, and broader cultural norms is likely to be crucial. A culture that embodies core values such as justice, equity, and fairness may increase the salience of goal frames conducive to value creation. Leadership styles, particularly those exemplifying servant leadership which focuses on the needs and emotional well-being of employees (cf. Wu et al., 2021) may lead to the same outcome. Yet, there is also a possibility that lower-level employees may adopt and champion beneficial goal frames, independent of direct managerial influence. Here, organizational identification (Section 3) might play a role. Future research should also examine the individual personality traits and attributes that encourage organizational members to support and spread specific goal frames.

Additionally, there has been work on dispositional and situational regulatory focus (Higgins, 1997, 1998) and its impact on interfirm relationships (Weber & Mayer, 2011), learning (Weber, 2017), acquisition decisions (Gamache et al., 2015), and firm stakeholder strategies (Gamache et al., 2020). This research examines how prevention- versus promotion-framed goals impact top management and lower-level managers' attention, emotions, behaviors, and strategic decisions, which influence firm-level outcomes. Again, this work has only begun to examine the impact of regulatory focus theory on firm performance, creating an opportunity for future research in this area.

Emotions. Despite emotions driving motivation, cognition, and behavior, and acting as a distinct influence in social interaction (Huy, 2012; van Knippenberg & van Kleef, 2016) that may affect organizational outcomes (Healey & Hodgkinson, 2017), behavioral strategy research disproportionally focuses on cognition. If emotions are considered, they are typically incorporated as impediments to effective decision-making (cf. Damasio, 1994; Rafaeli & Worline, 2001). However, more recent work showed that emotions may facilitate (interactive) decision-making in some contexts (e.g., Ehrig et al., 2022; Healey & Hodgkinson, 2017; Healey et al., 2018; Vuori & Huy, 2020).

Leadership research shows how leaders' affective displays – that is, expressions of leader mood or emotion observable to followers – motivate and mobile organizational members through emotional contagion (Elfenbein, 2014; Visser et al., 2013. Besides leaders' emotions, organizational members' emotions also play a crucial role in organizational change (Bartunek, Balogun, & Do, 2011). While most of these studies focus on employees' resistance to change and thus on managing and mitigating such resistance (Ford, Ford, & D'Amelio, 2008; Kiefer, 2005; Reger et al., 1994), recent work provides evidence that more positive emotions (including happiness, enjoyment, and enthusiasm) play a catalytic role in accelerating change (Bartunek et al., 2011; Kiefer, 2002; Liu & Perrewé, 2005).

Imagination. Although behavioral strategy research overlaps with fields like entrepreneurship and innovation, forward-looking, creative, or imaginative thinking tends to lie outside of the main research program (see Gavetti, 2012 and Winter, 2012). The reason arguably is that dominant approaches in behavioral strategy, such as the behavioral theory of the firm (Cyert & March, 1963), focus on the role of the past in shaping the future. Thus, the emphasis has been primarily on standard operating procedures, routines, organizational memory, and myopic, local search to explain why past firm behavior is the best predictor of future firm behavior. Another major approach to behavioral strategy, behavioral decision theory, assumes (like standard decision theory) that choice alternatives are essentially given. How actors generate (new) solution spaces under conditions of deficient knowledge and experience has generated less interest (e.g., Feduzi & Runde, 2014). This is surprising given that the construction of (new) decision situations is a key aspect of decision-making in March and Simon (1958).

The imaginative aspect of strategic decision-making is starting to garner renewed interest (e.g., Alvarez & Porac, 2020: 739). However, how decision-makers extract relevant information from the past and use it to predict and evaluate possible futures is not very clear. The emerging theory-based view in behavioral strategy (e.g., Felin & Zenger, 2017; Rindova & Martins, 2021) posits that decision-makers form theories much like scientists, which is anticipated in the psychology literature in George Kelly's "personal construct" theory (Kelly, 1970). The theory-based view characterizes valuable theories as novel, simple, falsifiable, and generalizable (Felin & Zenger, 2017), but does not offer further insight into how they are generated. The "conviction narrative theory" associated with David Tuckett (e.g., Johnson, Bilovich, & Tuckett, 2023) goes somewhat further. It suggests the psychological foundations of theories are "conviction narratives" that identify beliefs about relevant future variables and the mechanisms that link them. This perspective also shows how such narratives are subject to simulation, affective evaluation, and communication (cf. Rindova & Martins, 2022). As such, both the theory-based view and conviction narrative theory align with an older "scenario" tradition in strategy (see also Feduzi & Runde, 2014), which has made limited contact with behavioral strategy.

Predispositions. The notion of predisposition emphasizes the nonreflective aspect of human agency (Cardinale, 2018), and refers to the impromptu mobilization of skills in response to evolving situations, which is typically transmitted unconsciously via social practices. Nayak and colleagues further suggest predispositions are microfoundations of firm dynamic capabilities, as they provide a "tacitly honed capacity for improvisatory adaptive action that is unconsciously acquired in situ through extensive immersion in changing environmental conditions" (2020: 282).

The notion of predisposition helps in better understanding how firm constituents perceive and respond to environmental cues, processes that reflect perceptual sensitivities honed through prolonged exposure to both internal organizational dynamics and external environmental factors (Nayak et al., 2020). This view also underscores the importance of focusing on interfaces as opportunities for the unconscious transfer and expansion of predispositions. Shedding light on how interfaces facilitate the transfer and adaptation of predispositions can offer profound insights into how firms develop their dynamic capabilities and, thus, sustained competitive advantage.

The Where and When?

Routines. In Section 1, we mentioned a shift in the understanding of organizational routines, moving away from a view of them as static entities to dynamic, evolving processes (e.g., Feldman & Pentland, 2003). This evolution underscores the importance of human agency in renewing and adapting routines, challenging earlier notions of routines as mere repetition (Feldman, 2016; Parmigiani & Howard-Grenville, 2011).

While the study of routine dynamics traditionally focused on actions and their associations (Pentland et al., 2012), actions are inseparable from the agents performing them (D'Adderio & Pollock, 2014). As such, routines and routine dynamics provide fertile ground for behavioral strategy research, as they represent the main locus of interfaces. In this sense, behavioral strategy could both draw from and augment routine dynamics research by delving into routines as points of confluence for multiple agents' predispositions, cognitions, motivations, and actions (Weick & Roberts, 1993). Investigating routines as conduits of influence among various agents can clarify the relation between the action networks within routines and the individual actors involved. Furthermore, examining the intrinsic and extrinsic motivational factors, (beyond mere feedback mechanisms) that drive routine (re)production could illuminate when routines are more susceptible to change, which in turn affects organizational performance and adaptability (Abell, Felin, & Foss, 2008).

Artificial Intelligence. Simon (1995) not only developed the concept of bounded rationality but was also one of the pioneers in AI research in the 1950s. He believed that human behavior should be studied not just with psychology, but also modeled using computers (cf. also Newell & Simon, 1976). Today firms are increasingly using artificial intelligence (AI) – machines that perform cognitive functions typically associated with human minds (Nilsson, 1971) – across a range of operational and managerial tasks. The integration of AI is ushering in new forms of agency and new interfaces, redefining the boundaries of bounded rationality and transforming firms' experiential, structural, and relational systems in unprecedented ways (Kemp, 2023; Murray, Rhymer, & Sirmon, 2021).

From a cognitive perspective, AI-based algorithms are supercarriers of formal rationality because they can both optimize and improve themselves at an unprecedented speed (Lindebaum, Vesa, & den Hond, 2020). Delegating decision-making authority to AI can thus reduce firms' information processing costs resulting from the creation of vertical and horizontal information structures and the incentives to diminish information asymmetries. Moreover, AI has a significantly greater attentional capacity than humans, allowing for the simultaneous pursuit of multiple goals and, thereby, reducing the need to rely on priority rules for attention allocation (von Krogh, 2018). On the other hand, AI may exacerbate certain cognitive biases such as myopia (Balasubramanian, Ye, & Xu, 2022), and illusory causation (cf. Kiesler & Sproull, 1982). Delegating decision-making authority to AI can also hinder humans' reliance on perceptual sensitivity for discriminating between environmental stimuli and, thus, their capacity for improvisatory adaptive action (Daugherty & Wilson, 2018).

The evolving role of AI in mediating human interactions within organizations offers a novel area of investigation. AI systems, acting as intermediaries in communication processes, have the potential to significantly influence the flow and interpretation of information. They can also play a crucial role in governing sensemaking and social influence processes. For instance, AI systems can promote high-quality, "heedful" interrelations among firm constituents, fostering a shared understanding and facilitating concerted action (cf. McKee et al., 2023; Shirado & Christakis, 2020). Additionally, even though AI systems do not possess emotions, their ability to emulate human emotional responses can be instrumental in spreading positive emotions during crisis situations (cf. Han, Yin, & Zang, 2023; Prinz, 2022). However, there is a risk that AI might lead to increasingly uniform mental representations that suppress the requisite variety needed for adaptive shifts in information processing styles (cf. Steinbach, Gamache, & Johnson, 2019), potentially hindering firms' adaptability and eroding competitive advantage (Kemp, 2023).

Beyond their cognitive influence, AI and related technologies can also serve as motivational drivers. For instance, AI-driven performance monitoring systems can influence employee behavior by providing real-time feedback, thus fostering a more dynamic and responsive work environment (Tong et al., 2021). This aspect raises important questions about the potential of AI to facilitate both individual and organizational learning. However, complete delegation to AI systems might lead to reduced employee engagement and participation as well as encourage opportunistic behaviors, as employees could exploit the automated systems for personal gain, potentially at the expense of organizational goals. Such scenarios underscore the importance of maintaining a balance between AI automation and human involvement, ensuring that employees' accountability is preserved through some level of involvement with and control over relevant tasks (Raisch & Krakowski, 2021).

Network and Connections beyond the Organizational Boundaries. There is increasing recognition of the significant role played by social relationships and interfaces beyond firm boundaries in shaping strategists' decision-making and actions, and, as a consequence, firm behavior and outcomes (Tasselli et al., 2015; Westphal & Zajac, 2013). The extensive literature on board interlock ties, where board members concurrently serve on multiple corporate boards, shows that such ties act as conduits for social learning and the diffusion of strategies, practices, and norms between firms (e.g., Haunschild, 1993; McDonald & Westphal, 2003;). Relationships between firm leaders also were found to increase the likelihood of cooperative strategies (Gulati & Westphal, 1999).

Furthermore, social networks play a crucial role in shaping individual motivations and emotions (Burkhardt, 1994). For instance, individuals who are surrounded by pro-social (self-interested) others are more likely to become pro-social (self-interested) (Christakis & Fowler, 2013; Tsvetkova & Macy, 2015); and individuals who are surrounded by happy others are more likely to become happy (Fowler & Christakis, 2008). These networks also contribute to social identity formation, fulfilling fundamental human needs for belonging and serving as a foundation for identification (Walker & Lynn, 2013).

Recent research also focused on the psychological processes underpinning tie formation and their effective exploitation. Active pursuit or avoidance of certain relationships by individuals (Tasselli et al., 2015), and the interplay between network position and motivation, significantly impact both individual and firm-level outcomes (Tasselli et al., 2015). For instance, Reinholt, Pedersen, and Foss (2011) found that individuals' knowledge acquisition and provision were highest when both network centrality and autonomous motivation were high. This indicates that while structural position in a network is crucial, it is motivation that allows for leveraging network positions effectively (cf. Vissa, 2010).

Shedding further light on the motivational drivers leading specific firm participants to coalesce may also help to enhance our understanding of whether and
how distributed and shared cognition may coexist and interact (Stevenson &
Greenberg, 2000). While we know shared cognitions may not be a necessary
condition for coalescence (e.g., Fiol, 1994) (see Section 3), the extent to which
mental models need to be shared among participants to allow them to form
a coalition has not been examined.

Furthermore, trust, as an output of microlevel interactions within these
networks (cf. Emerson, 1976), acts as a resource that can be exchanged to
build and modify higher-level structures. Within firms, trust can serve as
a complementary or substitute governance mechanism to traditional authority
(Adler, 2001; Westphal & Zajac, 2013). At the same time, it may also undermine authority and reduce monitoring and supervision, particularly when arising from informal ties between superiors and subordinates (e.g., CEO and board
members) (Fredrickson, Hambrick, & Baumrin, 1988). Overall, by situating
interfaces into networks of structural ties beyond firm boundaries, behavioral
scholars may gain a better understanding of the origins of strategists' emotions,
motivations, and cognitions and formulate better predictions regarding their
subsequent impact on firm behavior and outcomes.

Uncertainty. Much work on behavioral decision theory is predicated on the
existence of "uncertainty," and this is largely true of behavioral strategy. Thus,
individuals and firms have to make choices among multiple alternatives with
different outcomes (Tversky & Kahneman, 1974; Simon, 1955), search "landscapes" they may know little about (Levinthal, 1997), and construct representations of those landscapes and their decision situations more generally
(Levinthal, 2011). However, it is not always clear what "uncertainty" means
in behavioral strategy. One reason is that scholars are often not forthcoming
about the kind of uncertainty, or, more broadly, the lack of knowledge
assumed. For example, a definition of uncertainty is seldom explicitly mentioned in the search literature derived from the behavioral theory of the firm
(e.g., Greve, 1998), although models that invoke "novelty" (e.g., Gavetti,
Levinthal, & Rivkin, 2005) seem to implicitly suggest that such search takes
place under conditions of partial ignorance about the future as well the present
"landscape."

Indeed, as one surveys the behavioral strategy literature, everything from
subjective probability (in Bayesian as well as non-Bayesian forms) to ambiguity
to sheer ignorance has been labeled as "uncertainty." For example, some key
contributions to behavioral decision theory (Tversky & Fox, 1995) explicitly
assume or posit conditions of risk. For example, much of the prospect theory
literature shows how framing gambles differently (notably, loss versus gain)

influences how risks are assessed, impacting choice behavior. Indeed, Gerd Gigerenzer argued that much of the heuristics and biases literature is fundamentally based on standard rational decision-making models, albeit with tweaks and add-ons (e.g., Gigerenzer, et al., 2011) Still, many others have used reasoning derived from such models to approach behavior under even radical uncertainty (i.e., decision-makers cannot describe future state spaces) (e.g., Feduzi & Runde, 2014; Mousavi & Gigerenzer, 2014).

Perhaps the reason behavioral strategy research has not typically clearly defined uncertainty is that it focuses on behaviors. Thus, it may loosely, but plausibly, assume that ambiguity leads to behaviors that reflect ambiguity, and that uncertainty leads to analogical reasoning in strategy-making (Gavetti et al., 2005). However, the microfoundations for such assumptions are not always clear. For example, there is much more to know about the psychological mechanisms producing analogies under different circumstances, or the extent to which cognitive bias findings derived in probabilistic settings are transferable to non-probabilistic situations (i.e., identifying decision alternatives and their outcomes is difficult).

These problems in behavioral strategy seem to stem from the lack of a clear understanding of decisions and behaviors under what is often called "Knightian uncertainty." Of course, behavioral strategy is not alone in lacking a clear understanding of Knightian uncertainty; the problem is a more general one in social science where multiple interpretations of such uncertainty have been proffered (Foss, 2023). However, behavioral strategy is championed because it attempts to grapple with real behaviors in realistic decision-making situations in a strategic context. If "Knightian uncertainty" means that our knowledge about the future often, perhaps usually, eludes quantification, it is incumbent upon behavioral strategy scholars to address such uncertainty.

While decision science and economics have developed several models of Knightian uncertainty, many of these are essentially tweaks of the basic Bayesian model of decision-making (Foss, 2023). Game theorists are also experimenting with modeling "unawareness" (i.e., there are parts of the state space that decision-makers are initially unaware of). However, none of these approaches make room for the role of imagination, stressed above as an important future research avenue in behavioral strategy. As argued in the section on Imagination (page 63), when the future does not exist, decision-makers exercise their imagination to be able to evaluate the desirability of potential outcomes. Such imagination often emerges as socially embedded narratives that respond to the existence of uncertainty in terms of including sense-making, outlining possible actions, and criteria for evaluating the future (Johnson, Bilovich, & Tuckett, 2023).

The Why and How?

As argued, most research in behavioral strategy is influenced heavily by Simon's conception of individuals as information processors, emphasizing organizational rules and routines to reduce complexity and treating organizations as unitary entities (e.g., Levinthal, 1997). This has resulted in a general lack of clarity with respect to the mechanisms that connect microlevel psychological aspects to firm-level behaviors and outcomes (cf. Christensen et al., 2021). Still, recent work has made significant strides in understanding the aggregation of individual choices and their impact on firm behavior and performance (see Cialdini & Goldstein, 2004).

Such research largely focuses on *intended aggregation mechanisms*, explicitly designed to align individual motivations, cognitions, and actions to enhance firm performance and competitive advantage, and including compliance via formal governance structures, social influence via power and communication, and political processes (e.g., Christensen & Knudsen, 2010; Csaszar & Eggers, 2013; Piezunka, Aggarwal, & Posen, 2022). "The basic premise in this line of research is that the organization has a fundamental role in aggregating choice functions, which characterize the organizational members' ability to pass judgment." (Christensen et al., 2021: 2). For instance, some work examines the effectiveness of different governance forms to mitigate the transaction costs ensuing from differences in participants' mental models as well as participants' self-interest (e.g., Foss & Weber, 2016) (Section 4). Studies also explore decision structures that promote endogenous adaptation and desired aggregate outcomes (e.g., Piezunka & Schilke, 2023), revealing that decentralized decision structures may engender unintended firm-level consequences and lead to suboptimal firm outcomes, even when individuals are unbiased (Christensen et al., 2021; Piezunka & Schilke, 2023). Furthermore, certain decision rules, such as averaging participants beliefs, albeit being particularly effective at aggregating individual knowledge into firm decisions, may ultimately be ineffective at fostering individual learning (Piezunka et al., 2022) and participation (Piezunka & Schilke, 2023).

Social norms may also have a role in connecting the micro and macro levels. Individuals often rely on social norms for guidance, especially in ambiguous situations where formal rules are not applicable (Cialdini, 2001). The influence of norms, ranging from subtly shaping behaviors to driving overt compliance, hinges on two factors: the prominence of these norms in an individual's consciousness and the alignment between different types of norms (Cialdini, 2003). Existing studies suggest that norms influence individual behavior when they are the focus of attention (cf. Hargadon, & Bechky, 2006). This happens when individuals are exposed to a certain stimulus for prolonged periods of time (Keizer, Lindenberg, & Steg, 2013) and intermittently (Bernstein, Shore, & Lazer, 2018). For instance, Weber and Murnighan (2008) demonstrate that when a single individual consistently exhibited prosocial behaviors, members came to perceive the norm as cooperative, becoming more willing to contribute themselves. This, however, implies that norms may explain "aggregation" only when they are consciously and prominently considered by individuals (Cialdini & Goldstein, 2004).

Social psychology literature offers relevant insights into *unintended aggregation mechanisms* that operate subconsciously, aligning individuals' motivations, emotions, and behaviors without deliberate design. Mechanisms like social contagion (i.e., the spontaneous distribution of ideas, emotions, attitudes, and behaviors among larger groups of people (Christakis & Fowler, 2013)) automatic activation through priming (i.e., information in the environment that makes related mental content accessible in a way that can potentially be used to guide judgment and behavior (Chartrand & Bargh 1999; Chen et al., 2021; Loersch & Payne, 2014)), and belief synchronization (i.e., an inherent tendency to select popular alternatives over unpopular ones (Denrell & Le Mens, 2017)) all subtly shape individuals' decisions and actions in a way that aggregates to organizational-level outcomes. Future research in behavioral strategy could delve into understanding these mechanisms and their interplay, which has often been overlooked. The next step of the behavioral strategy roadmap will consist of linking strategic choices, such as momentum, exploitative and explorative strategies, imitative strategies, and anticipatory strategies (e.g., forbearance) (cf. Greve, 2013; Andrevski & Miller, 2022), to their performance outcomes and understanding the role played by the aggregation mechanisms as drivers of such relationships.

Method Avenues

Although all empirical strategy research faces the core challenges of construct unobservability, measurement accuracy, and validity, these issues are particularly critical in behavioral strategy, as examining microfoundations of firm-level phenomena requires explicitly addressing these issues. It is imperative for research in behavioral strategy to examine the validity of constructs in foundational theories. A recent paper in the behavioral governance stream noted that asset specificity, the key construct driving holdup in TCE, is often difficult to quantify objectively and tends to be subjectively perceived by involved parties. These perceptions can be biased or even deliberately manipulated, leading to unexpected contractual stipulations that diverge from traditional TCE predictions (Weber & Coff, 2023). This emerging line of inquiry, examining the influence of perceptual factors on core theoretical propositions, underscores the need for a deeper understanding of how subjective interpretations can diminish construct validity.

Additionally, given the microfoundational nature of behavioral strategy research, another significant challenge is precisely defining both the level and unit of analysis in these studies. A recurrent theme has been the pursuit of both accuracy and depth in our understanding, coupled with the essential requirement for methodologies that are both reliable and consistent. We have also mentioned the importance of focusing on interfaces and context, advocating for empirical approaches that capture and account for the complex dynamics of real organizational settings as closely as possible. In the next section, our attention turns towards the potential of methodological and data pluralism. We will illustrate how this pluralism cannot only help address some of the existing challenges but also pave the way for progress in the field of behavioral strategy. We introduce a range of promising methods, followed by suggestions for their effective combination.

Multi-agent Experiments

Behavioral strategy scholars are increasingly adopting experimental methods as primary data-gathering and analysis techniques (Levine et al., 2023). Experiments offer multiple advantages, as they (1) are highly complementary to traditional modeling techniques in behavioral strategy (Billinger et al., 2014); (2) provide evidence of causal relationships (Greenberg & Tomlinson, 2004); and (3) explicate materials and instructions, easing replication (Croson, Anand, & Agarwal, 2007). Furthermore, with the growth of online crowdsourcing sites, such as Amazon Mechanical Turk and Prolific, conducting experiments has become more scalable. Many consider online experiments just as valid as lab experiments, even offering advantages such as subject diversity, market-like conditions, and the feasibility of longitudinal studies (Horton, Rand, & Zeckhauser, 2011; Paolacci, Chandler, & Ipeirotis, 2010; Rand, 2012). Yet, most online experiments involve very simple and often noninteractive tasks done independently (Giamattei et al., 2020), raising concerns about the generalizability of findings to real-world settings (Levitt & List, 2008).

New platforms allowing for synchronous and longitudinal experiments may address this issue (e.g., Mao et al., 2012), particularly when tasks and interactions are designed to enable participants' socialization, thus mimicking virtual work in actual organizations. Despite some criticism regarding the lack of realism and fidelity, virtual reality also has the potential to augment experimental settings, aligning them more closely with the organizational context under study (Brookes et al., 2020; Hubbard & Aguinis, 2023).

In choosing the experimental approach, behavioral scholars must carefully consider the trade-offs between accuracy and generalizability. This decision is compounded by the need to assess the applicability of findings on bounded rationality in strategic decision-making, particularly outside the controlled confines of laboratory settings (see Jussim, 2012). Field experiments may offer greater generalizability, especially when participant sampling allows for broader extrapolation. On the other hand, complementing online experiments with field-based case studies or subsequent firm-level data can complement the advantages of experiments with the richness of field data, offering realistic insights into the psychological underpinnings of firm competitive advantage.

Conversations, Narratives, and Natural Language Processing

The study of interaction and what we call "interfaces" above in behavioral strategy may also be furthered by conversation analysis, which uses management meeting textual data to analyze the situated processes of decision-making (Cooren, 2013; Cooren et al., 2014). This methodology hinges on the intertextual relationships between utterances (i.e., who says what, when, and how), in terms of such aspects as topic continuity, argumentative progression, and rhetorical devices, to gain a better understanding of what happens at the interface (e.g., König et al., 2018; Tuggle, Schnatterly, & Johnson, 2010). For instance, the application of conversation analysis has uncovered multiple discursive tactics that strategists employ to drive decision-making (Wodak et al., 2011).

Although this method has been largely adopted from a qualitative (ethnographic) perspective, the burgeoning field of computational linguistics – particularly machine learning and deep learning techniques for the analysis of textual data – presents opportunities to extend the scope and enhance the inferential reproducibility of conversation analysis. This expansion into computational techniques allows for scaling up the analysis to include a broader range of textual data beyond management meetings, such as text messages, emails, memos, presentation slides, etc. By incorporating interactions with organizational members at various hierarchical levels, this approach can provide a more comprehensive understanding of interactive processes at all organizational tiers and their cumulative impact on strategic decisions. Moreover, sentiment analysis of these conversations is an essential addition. By evaluating the emotions behind individual utterances, the combination of conversation and sentiment analysis can provide rich insights into firm-level implications of the interplay between participants' affective states, discursive tactics, and linguistic devices.

Earlier in this section, we pointed to the importance of narratives as key mental representations to imagine plausible futures and, thus, as means for sensemaking and decision-making under radical uncertainty (Chong & Tuckett, 2015). Topic modeling is a promising method to augment traditional narrative analysis, treating stories as the main unit of analysis (Riessman, 1993), and aiming at uncovering "semantically cohesive topics and their combination across document collections." (Evans & Aceves, 2016: 32). Algorithmically derived topic structures tend to be more transparent, reproducible, and less biased than pure qualitative analyses based on individual researchers' reading. Nevertheless, the structures generated by topic modeling are not self-explanatory and require careful interpretation. To enhance both reproducibility and interpretability, a promising approach is to present selections of prototypical text from the corpus corresponding to each identified topic, which may allow them to engage directly with the language used by individuals, facilitating a deeper understanding and a form of triangulation (Marchetti & Puranam, 2023). Additionally, integrating sentiment analysis into topic modeling could further refine the understanding of narratives. Sentiment analysis helps detect the emotional underpinnings within the narratives, offering insights into the mood and attitudes of the narrators. This combination can be especially powerful in understanding how strategists' narratives express more or less positive futures, shape organizational culture, and, in turn, influence decision-making processes.

Finally, algorithmic-aided text analysis is now regularly used in measuring various psychological constructs such as CEO motivation (regulatory focus) (Gamache et al., 2015), temporal focus (Nadkarni & Chen, 2014), justification content (Wade, Porac, & Pollock, 1997), and attention (Cho & Hambrick, 2006), primarily through the analysis of letters to shareholders in annual reports of publicly traded companies. The advent of sophisticated unsupervised machine learning techniques, including word embeddings and large language models, heralds new possibilities for measuring socio-cognitive constructs with greater reliability and accuracy. Word embeddings, which include methods like bag-of-words models, enable the extraction of semantic patterns from large text corpora, potentially revealing relationships between the cognitive frameworks of different organizational members (cf. Piezunka & Dahlander, 2015). By quantitatively analyzing word relationships in vector spaces, word embeddings can uncover implicit cognitive maps that guide organizational decision-making and strategy formulation, as well as provide insights into the collective cognitive alignment or divergence within an organization (cf. repertory grid techniques in Hodgkinson, Wright, and Anderson (2015)). Furthermore, large language models, such as GPT-4, are now capable of generating measures of semantic typicality (i.e., the degree of similarity of a text document to a concept) that closely mirror human judgment, which allows for considerable refinement with respect to measuring concepts like ambiguity, diversity, extremity, and polarization (Le Mens et al., 2023).

Visual Methods and Image Recognition

Nonparticipatory observation has been one of the most widely adopted methods in behavioral and social sciences where systems of categories have been developed to interpret and classify vocal, verbal, and nonverbal aspects of behaviors in social contexts, including static visual characteristics (e.g., race, sex, and facial appearance) and dynamic ones (e.g., gestures, facial expressions, and body language). Research suggests that visual cues significantly influence individual attention allocation, memory encoding, and decision-making processes (Mehta & Zhu, 2009; Tsay, 2021; Tversky, 1974), and that affective displays and subsequent emotional contagion were typically more salient through sight than other senses (Jack et al., 2016).

Nevertheless, compared to textual data analysis methods, approaches to analyze and interpret visual content are relatively less developed (Bell & Davison, 2013). Traditional visual content analysis relies on manual coding, leading to scalability and reliability issues. The advent of deep learning techniques in image processing and recognition presents opportunities for using visual data in behavioral strategy research. These advanced algorithmic methods offer scalability and reproducibility in analyzing visual content, surpassing the limitations of manual coding. Future studies in behavioral strategy could rely on these techniques to understand the types of visual cues that may provide information to facilitate effective decisions versus those that introduce errors in decision-making, as well as when these effects occur. Also, scholars could combine image and language processing models to investigate the salience of different sensory cues in judgment and decision-making processes under various situational circumstances (e.g., radical uncertainty) and whether primes or formal mechanisms can alter such salience (cf. Tsay, 2021). Another interesting avenue involves exploring how inconsistencies between different verbal and visual cues may influence dynamics at the interfaces. Such discrepancies can provide unique insights into the perceived authenticity and reliability of communicated messages, either facilitating or hindering organizational change. Thus, these methods offer a new approach to examining behavioral strategy questions that address some of the main issues typically faced in these studies.

Cognitive Maps and Geometric Spaces

In the late 1940s, Tolman discovered that animals assign locations to objects of experience in memory creating relationships between them in the form of a spatial maze (Tolman, 1948). Recent advancements show that similar map-like encoding mechanisms apply to nonspatial conceptual relationships, extending to imagination and abstract thinking (Horner et al., 2016; Kaplan, Schuck, & Doeller, 2017; Schiller et al., 2015). The hippocampal-entorhinal complex plays a key role in the organization of memory and the formation and navigation of such cognitive maps (Stoewer et al., 2023). These recent discoveries underscore the legitimacy and validity of geometric spaces and Euclidean distances to represent individual mental models and relationships between states in both empirical and computational studies in behavioral strategy (Hodgkinson et al., 2015). Intriguingly, this stream of work suggests mental maps are predictive: they represent each state in terms of its successor states (Stachenfeld et al., 2017). "Two states that predict similar future states will have similar representations, and two physically adjacent states that predict divergent future states will have dissimilar representations." (Stachenfeld et al., 2017: 1). This raises some crucial questions about how, for instance, decision-makers navigate solution spaces. Indeed, the focus of traditional NK models has been on similarity in terms of spatial proximity, whereby decision-makers progress through solution spaces by making incremental changes to current alternatives, often varying only one dimension at a time (Section 2). The novel perspective provided by contemporary neuroscience suggests a notion of similarity that aligns more closely with the notion of equifinality; with important implications for our traditional understanding of attention allocation and search (cf. Parker & Witteloostuijn, 2010).

Conclusion

Behavioral strategy has emerged as an increasingly influential voice in strategic management research as well as in the practice of strategy, with many consulting boutiques including behavioral strategy competencies in their skill sets. However, the field has been hampered by disconnected theorizing and by extremely broad definitions of the field, its explanatory mechanisms, and its scope. The main purpose of this Element is to renew the debate about these issues (beyond Powell et al., 2011) and to anchor behavioral strategy firmly in the bounded rationality microfoundations that gave initial impetus to the emerging field.

Thus, behavioral strategy falls at the intersection of typical strategic phenomena and an expanded set of psychological concepts, moving beyond just cognition to include elements such as intrinsic motivation, goals, and emotions. However, not all work at this intersection is behavioral strategy research, as a second requirement is that the approach is microfoundational. Furthermore, in this pursuit of microfoundations, we push researchers to move beyond psychological influences on just the CEO and top management team to examine psychological concepts in lower-level employees, which may impact their behavior and therefore firm performance.

We further emphasize the need for a better balance between generalizability and accuracy in behavioral strategy research. Central to this endeavor is the integration of social contextualization – encompassing the who, what, where, when, why, and how – into both theorizing and empirical analysis. Such an approach aims to develop theories with greater explanatory power of actual organizational behaviors and outcomes. It also requires a shift from perceiving firms as monolithic, often anthropomorphized, entities to adopting psychology-informed assumptions that emphasize individual motivations, cognitions, emotions, and behaviors and how these are altered via social interaction. This perspective will deepen our understanding of how situated social interactions among both intra- and interorganizational actors function as pivotal aggregation points and conduits between micro and macro levels. As a result, the thoughtful incorporation of psychological theories, constructs, and mechanisms into established strategy theories holds the potential to be theoretically generative, fostering novel predictions. These advancements pave the way for a more distinct characterization of the behavioral strategy subfield, simultaneously opening avenues for future research endeavors.

References

Abell, P., Felin, T., & Foss, N. 2008. Building micro-foundations for the routines, capabilities, and performance links. *Managerial and Decision Economics*, 29: 489–502.

Adler, P. S. 2001. Market, hierarchy, and trust: The knowledge economy and the future of capitalism. *Organization Science*, 12: 215–234.

Albert, S., & Whetten, D. A. 1985. Organizational identity. *Research in Organizational Behavior*, 7: 263–195.

Albert, S., Ashforth, B. E., & Dutton, J. E. 2000. Organizational identity and identification: Charting new waters and building new bridges. *Academy of Management Review*, 25: 13–17.

Alvarez, S. A., & Porac, J. 2020. Imagination, indeterminacy, and managerial choice at the limit of knowledge. *Academy of Management Review*, 45(4): 735–744.

Andrevski, G., & Miller, D. 2022. Forbearance: Strategic nonresponse to competitive attacks. *Academy of Management Review*, 47: 59–74.

Argote, L. 1999. *Organizational Learning: Creating, Retaining and Transferring Knowledge*. New York: Springer Science & Business Media.

Argote, L. & Greve, H. 2007. "A behavioral theory of the firm": 40 years and counting: Introduction and impact. *Organization Science*, 18: 337–349.

Ashforth, B. E., & Johnson, S. A. 2001. Which hat to wear? The relative salience of multiple identities in organizational contexts. In M. A. Hogg and D. J. Terry (eds.), *Social Identity Processes in Organizational Contexts* (pp. 31–48). Philadelphia: Psychology Press.

Ashforth, B. E., & Mael, F. 1989. Social identity theory and the organization. *Academy of Management Review*, 14: 20–39.

Ashforth, B. E., Harrison, S. H., & Corley, K. G. 2008. Identification in organizations: An examination of four fundamental questions. *Journal of Management*, 34(3): 325–374.

Audia, P. G., & Greve, H. R. 2006. Less likely to fail: Low performance, firm size, and factory expansion in the shipbuilding industry. *Management Science*, 52: 83–94.

Barr, P. S., Stimpert, J. L., & Huff, A. S. 1992. Cognitive change, strategic action, and organizational renewal. *Strategic Management Journal*, 13: 15–36.

Baer, M., Dirks, K. T., & Nickerson, J. A. 2013. Microfoundations of strategic problem formulation. *Strategic Management Journal*, 34: 197–214.

Balasubramanian, N., Ye, Y., & Xu, M. 2022. Substituting human decision-making with machine learning: Implications for organizational learning. *Academy of Management Review*, 47(3): 448–465.

Balogun, J., & Johnson, G. 2004. Organizational restructuring and middle manager sensemaking. *Academy of Management Journal*, 47: 523–549.

Barnes, J. H. 1984. Cognitive biases and their impact on strategic planning. *Strategic Management Journal*, 5: 129–137.

Bartunek, J. M. 1984. Changing interpretive schemes and organizational restructuring: The example of a religious order. *Administrative Science Quarterly*, 29: 355–372.

Bartunek, J. M., Balogun, J., & Do, B. 2011. Considering planned change anew: Stretching large group interventions strategically, emotionally, and meaningfully. *The Academy of Management Annals*, 5(1): 1–52.

Bartunek, J. M., & Moch, M. K. 1987. First-order, second-order, and third-order change and organization development interventions: A cognitive approach. *Journal of Applied Behavioral Science*, 23: 483–500.

Bass, A. E., Pfarrer, M. D., Milosevic, I., & Titus Jr, V. K. 2023. Better to be loved by some? Firm flaunting as an impression management strategy. *Academy of Management Review*, 48: 292–312.

Baum, J. A., Li, S. X., & Usher, J. M. 2000. Making the next move: How experiential and vicarious learning shape the locations of chains' acquisitions. *Administrative Science Quarterly*, 45: 766–801.

Baumann, O., Schmidt, J., & Stieglitz, N. 2019. Effective search in rugged performance landscapes: A review and outlook. *Journal of Management*, 45: 285–318.

Bell, E., & Davison, J. 2013. Visual management studies: Empirical and theoretical approaches. *International Journal of Management Reviews*, 15: 167–184.

Benner, M. J., & Tripsas, M. 2012. The influence of prior industry affiliation on framing in nascent industries: The evolution of digital cameras. *Strategic Management Journal*, 33(3): 277–302.

Bernstein, E., Shore, J., & Lazer, D. 2018. How intermittent breaks in interaction improve collective intelligence. *Proceedings of the National Academy of Sciences*, 115(35): 8734–8739.

Billinger, S., Stieglitz, N., & Schumacher, T. R. 2014. Search on rugged landscapes: An experimental study. *Organization Science*, 25(1): 93–108.

Bingham C. B. & Eisenhardt, K. M. 2011. Rational heuristics: The "simple rules" strategists learn from their process experiences. *Strategic Management Journal*, 32: 1437–1464.

Bitektine, A. 2011. Toward a theory of social judgments of organizations: The case of legitimacy, reputation, and status. *Academy of Management Review*, 36(1): 151–179.

Bosse, D. A., & Phillips, R. A. 2016. Agency theory and bounded self-interest. *Academy of Management Review*, 41(2): 276–297.

Bougon, M., Weick, K., & Binkhorst, D. 1977. Cognition in organizations: An analysis of the Utrecht Jazz Orchestra. *Administrative Science Quarterly*, 22: 606–639.

Bouquet, C., & Birkinshaw, J. 2008. Managing power in the multinational corporation: How low-power actors gain influence. *Journal of Management*, 34: 477–508.

Bouquet, C., Morrison, A., & Birkinshaw, J. 2009. International attention and multinational enterprise performance. *Journal of International Business Studies*, 40: 108–131.

Boivie, S., Lange, D., McDonald, M. L., & Westphal, J. D. 2011. Me or we: The effects of CEO organizational identification on agency costs. *Academy of Management Journal*, 54(3): 551–576.

Boje, D. M. 1991. Consulting and change in the storytelling organisation. *Journal of Organizational Change Management*, 4(3): 7–17.

Boje, D. M. (2017). The storytelling organization: A study of story performance in an office-supply firm. In S. Minahan & J. Wolfram Cox (eds.), *The Aesthetic Turn in Management* (pp. 211–231). New York: Routledge.

Bouchikhi, H., & Kimberly, J. R. 2003. Escaping the identity trap. *MIT Sloan Management Review*, 44(3): 20–26.

Brewer, M. B. 1991. The social self: On being the same and different at the same time. *Personality and Social Psychology Bulletin*, 17(5): 475–482.

Brewer, M. B., & Gardner, W. 1996. Who is this" We"? Levels of collective identity and self representations. *Journal of Personality and Social Psychology*, 71(1): 83–93.

Bridoux, F., Coeurderoy, R., & Durand, R. 2011. Heterogeneous motives and the collective creation of value. *Academy of Management Review*, 36: 711–730.

Bromiley, P. 2010. Looking at prospect theory. *Strategic Management Journal*, 31: 1357–1370.

Bromiley, P., Koumakhov, R., Rousseau, D. M., & Starbuck, W. H. 2019. The challenges of March and Simon's *Organizations*: Introduction to the special issue. *Journal of Management Studies*, 56: 1517–1526.

Bromiley, P., & Rau, D. 2022. Some problems in using prospect theory to explain strategic management issues. *Academy of Management Perspectives*, 36: 125–141.

Brookes, J., Warburton, M., Alghadier, M., Mon-Williams, M., & Mushtaq, F. 2020. Studying human behavior with virtual reality: The unity experiment framework. *Behavior Research Methods*, 52: 455–463.

Brown, A. D., Stacey, P., & Nandhakumar, J. 2008. Making sense of sensemaking narratives. *Human Relations*, 61: 1035–1062.

Burkhardt, M. E. 1994. Social interaction effects following a technological change: A longitudinal investigation. *Academy of Management Journal*, 37(4): 869–898.

Burkhard, B., Sirén, C., van Essen, M., Grichnik, D. & Shepherd, D. A. 2022. Nothing ventured, nothing gained: A meta-analysis of CEO overconfidence, strategic risk taking, and performance'. *Journal of Management*, 49(8): 2629–2666. https://doi.org/01492063221110203.

Burton, R. M., & Obel, B. 2018. The science of organizational design: Fit between structure and coordination. *Journal of Organization Design*, 7: 1–13.

Busenitz, L. W., & Barney, J. B. 1997. Differences between entrepreneurs and managers in large organizations: Biases and heuristics in strategic decision-making. *Journal of Business Venturing*, 12(1): 9–30.

Cardinale, I. 2018. Beyond constraining and enabling: Toward new microfoundations for institutional theory. *Academy of Management Review*, 43: 132–155.

Chaiken, S., & Trope, Y. 1999. *Dual-process Theories in Social Psychology*. Guilford Press. Chandler, A. D. 1962. *Strategy and Structure*. Boston: MIT Press.

Chartrand, T. L., & Bargh, J. A. 1999. The chameleon effect: The perception–behavior link and social interaction. *Journal of Personality and Social Psychology*, 76: 893–910.

Chen, G., Crossland, C., & Luo, S. 2015. Making the same mistake all over again: CEO overconfidence and corporate resistance to corrective feedback. *Strategic Management Journal*, 36: 1513–1535.

Chen, X., Latham, G. P., Piccolo, R. F., & Itzchakov, G. 2021. An enumerative review and a meta-analysis of primed goal effects on organizational behavior. *Applied Psychology*, 70: 216–253.

Cho, T. S., & Hambrick, D. C. 2006. Attention as the mediator between top management team characteristics and strategic change: The case of airline deregulation. *Organization Science*, 17: 453–469.

Chong, K., & Tuckett, D. 2015. Constructing conviction through action and narrative: How money managers manage uncertainty and the consequence for financial market functioning. *Socio-Economic Review*, 13: 309–330.

Christakis, N. A. & Fowler, J. H. 2013. Social contagion theory: Examining dynamic social networks and human behavior. *Statistical Medicine*, 32: 556–577.

Christensen, M. & Knudsen, T. 2010. Design of decision-making organizations. *Management Science*, 56: 71–89.

Christensen, M., Dahl, C. M., Knudsen, T., & Warglien, M. 2021. Context and aggregation: An experimental study of bias and discrimination in organizational decisions. *Organization Science*, 34: 2163–2181.

Christianson, M. K., Farkas, M. T., Sutcliffe, K. M., & Weick, K. E. 2009. Learning through rare events: Significant interruptions at the Baltimore & Ohio Railroad Museum. *Organization Science*, 20: 846–860.

Cialdini R. B. 2001. *Influence: Science and Practice.* Boston, MA: Allyn & Bacon. 4th ed.

Cialdini, R. B. 2003. Crafting normative messages to protect the environment. *Current Directions in Psychological Science*, 12: 105–109.

Cialdini, R. B., & Goldstein, N. J. 2004. Social influence: Compliance and conformity. *Annual Review of Psychology*, 55: 591–621.

Cooren, F. 2013. *Interacting and Organizing: Analyses of a Management Meeting.* London: Routledge.

Cooren, F., Vaara, E., Langley, A., & Tsoukas, H., eds. 2014. *Language and Communication at Work: Discourse, Narrativity, and Organizing* (Volume 4). Oxford: Oxford University press.

Corley, K. G., & Gioia, D. A. 2004. Identity ambiguity and change in the wake of a corporate spin-off. *Administrative Science Quarterly*, 49(2): 173–208.

Cornelissen, J. P., & Werner, M. D. 2014. Putting framing in perspective: A review of framing and frame analysis across the management and organizational literature. *Academy of Management Annals*, 8(1): 181–235.

Croson, R., Anand, J., & Agarwal, R. 2007. Using experiments in corporate strategy research. *European Management Review*, 4: 173–181.

Csaszar, F. A. & Eggers, J. P. 2013. Organizational decision making: An information aggregation view. *Management Science*, 59: 2257–2277.

Cuevas-Rodríguez, G., Gomez-Mejia, L. R., & Wiseman, R. M. (2012). Has agency theory run its course?: Making the theory more flexible to inform the management of reward systems. *Corporate Governance: An International Review*, 20(6): 526–546.

Cyert, R. M., & DeGroot, M. H. 1974. Rational expectations and Bayesian analysis. *Journal of Political Economy*, 82: 521–536.

Cyert, R. M., & March, J. G. 1963. *A Behavioral Theory of the Firm.* Englewood Cliffs, NJ: Prentice-Hall.

D'adderio, L., & Pollock, N. 2014. Performing modularity: Competing rules, performative struggles and the effect of organizational theories on the organization. *Organization Studies*, 35(12): 1813–1843.

Daft, R. L., & Weick, K. E. 1984. Toward a model of organizations as interpretation systems. *Academy of Management Review*, 9: 284–295.

Damasio A. R. 1994. *Descartes' Error: Emotion, Reason, and the Human Brain*. New York: Grosset/Putnam.

Das, T. K., & Teng, B. S. 1999. Cognitive biases and strategic decision processes: An integrative perspective. *Journal of Management Studies*, 36: 757–778.

Daugherty, P. R., & Wilson, H. J. 2018. *Human + Machine: Reimagining Work in the Age of AI*. Boston, MA: Harvard Business Press.

Davidson, E. J. 2002. Technology frames and framing: A socio-cognitive investigation of requirements determination. *MIS Quarterly*, 26: 329–358.

Davis, J. H. &, Schoorman, F. D., & Donaldson L. 1997. Toward a stewardship theory of management. *Academy of Management Review*, 22(1): 20–47.

Daw, N. D., Gershman, S. J., Seymour, B., Dayan, P, & Dolan, R. J. 2011. Model-based influences on humans' choices and striatal prediction errors. *Neuron*, 69: 1204–1215.

Dearborn, D. C., & Simon, H. A. 1958. Selective perception: A note on the departmental identifications of executives. *Sociometry*, 21: 140–144.

Deci, E. L., & Ryan, R. M. 2012. Self-determination theory. *Handbook of Theories of Social Psychology*, 1(20): 416–436.

Denrell, J., & Le Mens, G. 2017. Information sampling, belief synchronization, and collective illusions. *Management Science*, 63: 528–547.

Denrell, J., & March, J. G. 2001. Adaptation as information restriction: The hot stove effect. *Organization Science*, 12: 523–538.

Devers, C. E., Cannella Jr, A. A., Reilly, G. P., & Yoder, M. E. 2007. Executive compensation: A multidisciplinary review of recent developments. *Journal of Management*, 33: 1016–1072.

Dougherty, D., Borrelli, L., Munir, K., & O'Sullivan, A. 2000. Systems of organizational sensemaking for sustained product innovation. *Journal of Engineering and Technology Management*, 17: 321–355.

Dreyfus, H. L. 2002. Intelligence without representation–Merleau-Ponty's critique of mental representation The relevance of phenomenology to scientific explanation. *Phenomenology and the Cognitive Sciences*, 1(4): 367–383.

Dreyfus, H. L. 2014. *Skillful Coping: Essays on the Phenomenology of Everyday Perception and Action*. Oxford: Oxford University Press.

Dutton, J. E., & Ashford, S. J. 1993. Selling issues to top management. *Academy of Management Review*, 18: 397–428.

Dutton, J. E., Dukerich, J. M., & Harquail, C. V. 1994. Organizational images and member identification. *Administrative Science Quarterly*, 2: 239–263.

Dutton, J. E., Fahey, L., & Narayanan, V. K. 1983. Toward understanding strategic issue diagnosis. *Strategic Management Journal*, 4: 307–323.

Eggers, J. P. & Kaplan, S. 2013. Cognition and capabilities: A multi-level perspective. *Academy of Management Annals*, 7: 295–340.

Ehrig, T. & Foss, N. J. 2020. Risk, uncertainty, and COVID-19 strategies. https://quillette.com/2020/05/04/risk-uncertainty-and-covid-19-strategies/

Ehrig, T., & Foss, N. J. 2022. Unknown unknowns and the treatment of firm-level adaptation in strategic management research. *Strategic Management Review*, 3: 1–24.

Ehrig, T., Manjaly, J., Singh, A., & Sunder, S. 2022. Adaptive rationality in strategic interaction: Do emotions regulate thinking about others?. *Strategy Science*, 7: 330–349.

Eisenhardt, K. M. 1989. Making fast strategic decisions in high-velocity environments. *Academy of Management Journal*, 32: 543–576.

Eisenhardt, K. M., & Bourgeois III, L. J. 1988. Politics of strategic decision making in high-velocity environments: Toward a midrange theory. *Academy of Management Journal*, 31: 737–770.

Elfenbein, H. A. 2014. The many faces of emotional contagion: An affective process theory of affective linkage. *Organizational Psychology Review*, 4: 326–362.

Elsbach, K. D. 2003. Organizational perception management. *Research in Organizational Behavior*, 25: 297–332.

Elsbach, K. D., Barr, P. S., & Hargadon, A. B. 2005. Identifying situated cognition in organizations. *Organization Science*, 16(4): 422–433.

Elsbach, K. D., & Kramer, R. M. 1996. Members' responses to organizational identity threats: Encountering and countering the Business Week rankings. *Administrative Science Quarterly*, 41: 442–476.

Emerson, R. M. 1976. Social exchange theory. *Annual Review of Sociology*, 2(1): 335–362.

Evans, J. A., & Aceves, P. 2016. Machine translation: Mining text for social theory. *Annual Review of Sociology*, 42: 21–50.

Fahey, L., & Narayanan, V. K. 1989. Linking changes in revealed causal maps and environmental change: An empirical study. *Journal of Management Studies*, 26: 361–378.

Fama, E. F., & Jensen, M. C. 1983. Separation of ownership and control. *Journal of Law and Economics*, 26: 301–325.

Feduzi, A. & Runde, J. 2014. Uncovering unknown unknowns: Towards a Baconian approach to management decision-making. *Organizational Behavior and Human Decision Processes*, 124: 268–283.

Feldman, M. S. 2016. Routines as process Past, present, and future. In J. A. Howard-Grenville, C. Rerup, A. Langley, & H. Tsoukas (eds.), *Organizational*

Routines: How they are Created, Maintained, and Changed (pp. 23–46). Oxford: Oxford University Press.

Feldman, M. S., & Pentland, B. T. 2003. Reconceptualizing organizational routines as a source of flexibility and change. *Administrative Science Quarterly*, 48: 94–118.

Felin, T. & Foss, N. J. 2005. Strategic Organization: A field in search of microfoundations. *Strategic Organization*, 3: 441–455.

Felin, T., Foss, N. J., & Ployhart, R. E. 2015. The microfoundations movement in strategy and organization theory. *Academy of Management Annals*, 9: 575–632.

Felin, T., & Zenger, T. R. 2017. The theory-based view: Economic actors as theorists. *Strategy Science*, 2(4): 258–271.

Fiol, C. M. 1991. Managing culture as a competitive resource: An identity-based view of sustainable competitive advantage. *Journal of Management*, 17(1): 191–211.

Fiol, C. M. 1994. Consensus, diversity, and learning in organizations. *Organization Science*, 5(3): 403–420.

Fiol, C. M. 2001. Revisiting an identity-based view of sustainable competitive advantage. *Journal of Management*, 27(6): 691–699.

Fischhoff, B. 1996. The real world: what good is it?. *Organizational Behavior and Human Decision Processes*, 65: 232–248.

Fiske, S. T., & Taylor, S. E. 1984. *Social Cognition*. New York: Random House.

Fiss, P. C., & Zajac, E. J. 2004. The diffusion of ideas over contested terrain: The (non) adoption of a shareholder value orientation among German firms. *Administrative Science Quarterly*, 49(4): 501–534.

Forbes, D. P. (2005). Managerial determinants of decision speed in new ventures. *Strategic Management Journal*, 26(4): 355–366.

Ford, J. D., & Baucus, D. A. 1987. Organizational adaptation to performance downturns: An interpretation-based perspective. *Academy of Management Review*, 12(2): 366–380.

Ford J., Ford L., D'Amelio A. 2008. Resistance to change: The rest of the story. *Academy of Management Review*, 33(2): 362–377.

Foss, N., & Stea, D. 2014. Putting a realistic theory of mind into agency theory: Implications for reward design and management in principal-agent relations. *European Management Review*, 11: 101–116.

Foss, N. J. 2001. Bounded rationality in the economics of organization: Present use and (some) future possibilities. *Journal of Management & Governance*, 5: 401–425.

Foss, N. J. 2003. The rhetorical dimensions of bounded rationality: Herbert A. Simon and organizational economics. In S. Rizzello (ed.), *Cognitive Paradigms in Economics* (pp. 170–171). London: Routledge.

Foss, N. J. 2020. Behavioral strategy and the Covid-19 disruption. *Journal of Management*, 46: 1322–1329.

Foss, N. J. 2023. Expanding the boundaries of rationality": Knightian uncertainty and the limitations of the Savage Heuristic. *European Management Review*, 20(4): 626–631.

Foss, N. J. & Hallberg, N. 2014. How symmetrical assumptions facilitate theoretical advance in strategic management: The case of the resource-based view. *Strategic Management Journal*, 35: 903–913.

Foss, N. J. & Lindenberg, S. 2013. Strategy in a goal-framing perspective. *Academy of Management Perspectives*, 27: 85–102.

Foss, N. J., & Weber, L. 2016. Moving opportunism to the back seat: Bounded rationality, costly conflict, and hierarchical forms. *Academy of Management Review*, 41: 61–79.

Fowler, J. H. & Christakis, N. A. 2008. Dynamic spread of happiness in a large social network: Longitudinal analysis over 20 years in the Framingham Heart Study. *British Medical Journal*, 337, a2338.

Fredrickson, J. W., Hambrick, D. C., & Baumrin, S. 1988. A model of CEO dismissal. *Academy of Management Review*, 13: 255–270.

Friedman, M. & Savage, L. J. 1948. Utility analysis of choices involving risk. *Journal of Political Economy*, 56: 279–304.

Gaba, V., & Joseph, J. 2013. Corporate structure and performance feedback: Aspirations and adaptation in M-form firms. *Organization Science*, 24: 1102–1119.

Galbraith, J. 1973. *Designing Complex Organizations*. Reading, MA: Addison-Wesley.

Galbraith J. R. 1977. *Organization Design*. Reading, MA: Addison-Wesley.

Gamache, D. L., McNamara, G., Mannor, M. J., & Johnson, R. E. (2015). Motivated to acquire? The impact of CEO regulatory focus on firm acquisitions. *Academy of Management Journal*, 58: 1261–1282.

Gamache, D. L., Neville, F., Bundy, J., & Short, C. E. (2020). Serving differently: CEO regulatory focus and firm stakeholder strategy. *Strategic Management Journal*, 41: 1305–1335.

Gavetti, G. 2012. Perspective—Toward a behavioral theory of strategy. *Organization Science*, 23: 267–285.

Gavetti, G., & Levinthal, D. 2000. Looking forward and looking backward: Cognitive and experiential search. *Administrative Science Quarterly*, 45: 113–137.

Gavetti, G., Levinthal, D., & Ocasio, W. 2007. Perspective—Neo-Carnegie: The Carnegie school's past, present, and reconstructing for the future. *Organization Science*, 18: 523–536.

Gavetti, G., Greve, H. R., Levinthal, D. A., & Ocasio, W. 2012. The behavioral theory of the firm: Assessment and prospects. *Academy of Management Annals*, 6: 1–40.

Gavetti, G., Levinthal, D. A. & Rivkin, J. W. 2005. Strategy making in novel and complex worlds: The power of analogy. *Strategic Management Journal*, 26: 691–712.

Gephart, R. P., Topal, C. & Zhang, Z. 2010. Future-oriented sensemaking: Temporalities and institutional legitimation. In T. Hernes & S. Maitlis (eds.), *Process, Sensemaking, and Organizing* (pp. 275–302). Oxford: Oxford University Press.

Ghoshal, S., & Moran, P. 1996. Bad for practice: A critique of the transaction cost theory. *Academy of Management Review*, 21(1): 13–47.

Giamattei, M., Yahosseini, K. S., Gächter, S., & Molleman, L. 2020. LIONESS Lab: A free web-based platform for conducting interactive experiments online. *Journal of the Economic Science Association*, 6: 95–111.

Gick, M. L. & Holyoak, K. G. 1983. Schema induction and analogical transfer. *Cognitive Psychology*, 15: 1–38.

Gigerenzer, G. & Gaissmaier, W. 2011. Heuristic decision making. *Annual Review of Psychology*, 62: 451–482.

Gigerenzer, G. & Goldstein, D. G. 1996. Reasoning the fast and frugal way: Models of bounded rationality. *Psychological Review*, 103: 650–669.

Gigerenzer, G., Hertwig, R., & Pachur, T., eds. 2011. *Heuristics: The Foundations of Adaptive Behavior*. Oxford, UK: Oxford University Press.

Gigerenzer, G., Todd, P. M. & The ABC Research Group. 1999. *Simple Heuristics that Make Us Smart*. Oxford: Oxford University Press.

Gilbert, C. G. 2006. Change in the presence of residual fit: Can competing frames coexist? *Organization Science*, 17(1): 150–167.

Gioia, D. A., & Chittipeddi, K. 1991. Sensemaking and sensegiving in strategic change initiation. *Strategic Management Journal*, 12: 433–448.

Gioia, D. A., Corley, K. G., & Hamilton, A. L. 2013. Seeking qualitative rigor in inductive research: Notes on the Gioia methodology. *Organizational Research Methods*, 16(1): 15–31.

Goffman, E. 1974. *Frame Analysis: An Essay on the Organization of Experience*. Boston, MA: North Eastern University Press.

Gottschalg, O. & Zollo, M. 2007. Interest alignment and competitive advantage. *Academy of Management Review*, 32: 418–437.

Greenberg, J., & Tomlinson, E. C. 2004. Situated experiments in organizations: Transplanting the lab to the field. *Journal of Management*, 30: 703–724.

Greve, H. 1998. Performance, Aspirations, and Risky Organizational Change. *Administrative Science Quarterly*, 43: 58–86.

Greve, H. R. 2013. Microfoundations of management: Behavioral strategies and levels of rationality in organizational action. *Academy of Management Perspectives*, 27: 103–119.

Greve, H. R. 2003. A behavioral theory of R&D expenditures and innovations: Evidence from shipbuilding. *Academy of Management Journal*, 46: 685–702.

Gulati, R., & Westphal, J. D. 1999. Cooperative or controlling? The effects of CEO-board relations and the content of interlocks on the formation of joint ventures. *Administrative Science Quarterly*, 44: 473–506.

Hambrick, D. C. 2007. Upper echelons theory: An update. *Academy of Management Review*, 32: 334–343.

Hambrick, D. C., & Crossland, C. 2018. A strategy for behavioral strategy: Appraisal of small, midsize, and large tent conceptions of this embryonic community. In M. Augier, C. Fang, & V. P. Rindova (eds.), *Behavioral Strategy in Perspective* (Vol. 39, pp. 23–39). Bingley, UK: Emerald.

Hambrick, D. C., & Mason, P. A. 1984. Upper echelons: The organization as a reflection of its top managers. *Academy of Management Review*, 9: 193–206.

Hambrick, D. C., Werder, A. V., & Zajac, E. J. 2008. New directions in corporate governance research. *Organization Science*, 19: 381–385.

Han, E., Yin, D., & Zhang, H. 2023. Bots with feelings: should AI agents express positive emotion in customer service? *Information Systems Research*, 34: 1296–1311.

Hargadon, A. B., & Bechky, B. A. 2006. When collections of creatives become creative collectives: A field study of problem solving at work. *Organization Science*, 17: 484–500.

Haslam, S. A., & Ellemers, N. 2005. Social identity in industrial and organizational psychology: Concepts, controversies and contributions. *International Review of Industrial and Organizational Psychology*, 20: 39–118.

Haunschild, P. R. 1993. Interorganizational imitation: The impact of interlocks on corporate acquisition activity. *Administrative Science Quarterly*, 38: 564–592.

Healey, M. P., & Hodgkinson, G. P. 2017. Making strategy hot. *California Management Review*, 59(3): 109–134.

Healey, M. P., Hodgkinson, G. P., & Massaro, S. 2017. Emotion regulation in organizations: Integrating neural and social processes. In *Academy of Management Proceedings* (Vol. 2017, No. 1, p. 16741). Briarcliff Manor: Academy of Management.

Helfat, C. E. & Peteraf, M. A. 2015. Managerial cognitive capabilities and the microfoundations of dynamic capabilities. *Strategic Management Journal*, 36: 831–850.

Higgins, E. T. 1997. Beyond pleasure and pain. *American Psychologist*, 52(12): 1280.

Higgins, E. T. 1998. Promotion and prevention: Regulatory focus as a motivational principle. *Advances in Experimental Social Psychology*, 30: 1–46.

Hill, R. C., & Levenhagen, M. 1995. Metaphors and mental models: Sensemaking and sensegiving in innovative and entrepreneurial activities. *Journal of Management*, 21(6): 1057–1074.

Hodgkinson, G. P., Maule, A. J., & Bown, N. J. 2004. Causal cognitive mapping in the organizational strategy field: A comparison of alternative elicitation procedures. *Organizational Research Methods*, 7: 3–26.

Hodgkinson, G. P. 1997. The cognitive analysis of competitive structures: A review and critique. *Human Relations*, 50: 625–654.

Hodgkinson, G. P., Bown, N. J., Maule, A. J., Glaister, K. W., & Pearman, A. D. 1999. Breaking the frame: An analysis of strategic cognition and decision making under uncertainty. *Strategic Management Journal*, 20: 977–985.

Hodgkinson, G. P., Burkhard, B., Foss, N. J. et al. 2023. The heuristics and biases of top managers: Past, present, and future. *Journal of Management Studies*, 60(5): 1033–1063.

Hodgkinson, G. P., & Healey, M. P. 2008. Cognition in organizations. *Annual Review of Psychology*, 59: 387–417.

Hodgkinson, G. P. & Healey, M. P. 2011. Psychological foundations of dynamic capabilities: Reflexion and reflection in strategic management. *Strategic Management Journal*, 32: 1500–1516.

Hodgkinson, G. P., & Johnson, G. 1994. Exploring the mental models of competitive strategists: The case for a processual approach. *Journal of Management Studies*, 31: 525–552.

Hodgkinson, G. P., Wright, R. P., & Anderson, J. 2015. Emotionalizing strategy research with the repertory grid technique: Modifications and extensions to a robust procedure for mapping strategic knowledge. *Advances in Strategic Management*, 32: 505–547.

Hogg, M. A., & Terry, D. J. 2000. The dynamic, diverse, and variable faces of organizational identity. *Academy of Management Review*, 251: 150–152.

Holmes Jr, R. M., Bromiley, P., Devers, C. E., Holcomb, T. R., & McGuire, J. B. 2011. Management theory applications of prospect theory: Accomplishments, challenges, and opportunities. *Journal of Management*, 37: 1069–1107.

Horner, A. J., Bisby, J. A., Zotow, E., Bush, D., & Burgess, N. 2016. Grid-like processing of imagined navigation. *Current Biology*, 26: 842–847.

Horton, J. J., Rand, D. G., & Zeckhauser, R. J. 2011. The online laboratory: Conducting experiments in a real labor market. *Experimental Economics*, 14: 399–425.

Hoskisson, R. E., Chirico, F., Zyung, J., & Gambeta, E. 2017. Managerial risk taking: A multitheoretical review and future research agenda. *Journal of Management*, 43: 137–169.

Hubbard, T. D., & Aguinis, H. 2023. Conducting phenomenon-driven research using virtual reality and the metaverse. *Academy of Management Discoveries*, 9: 408–415.

Huff, A. S. 1982. Industry influences on strategy reformulation. *Strategic Management Journal*, 3: 119–131.

Huff, A. S. 1990. *Mapping Strategic Thought*. New York: John Wiley & Sons.

Hung, S. C. 2005. The plurality of institutional embeddedness as a source of organizational attention differences. *Journal of Business Research*, 58: 1543–1551.

Husted, B. W., & Folger, R. 2004. Fairness and transaction costs: The contribution of organizational justice theory to an integrative model of economic organization. *Organization Science*, 15: 719–729.

Huy, Q. N. 2012. Emotions in strategic organization: Opportunities for impactful research. *Strategic Organization*, 10: 240–247.

Huy, Q. N., Corley, K. G., & Kraatz, M. S. 2014. From support to mutiny: Shifting legitimacy judgments and emotional reactions impacting the implementation of radical change. *Academy of Management Journal*, 57: 1650–1680.

Jack, R. E., Sun, W., Delis, I., Garrod, O. G. B., & Schyns, P. G. 2016. Four not six: Revealing culturally common facial expressions of emotion. *Journal of Experimental Psychology: General*, 145: 708–730.

Jackson, S. E., & Dutton, J. E. 1988. Discerning threats and opportunities. *Administrative Science Quarterly*, 33: 370–387.

Jay, J. 2013. Navigating paradox as a mechanism of change and innovation in hybrid organizations. *Academy of Management Journal*, 56: 137–159.

Jensen, M. C. & Meckling W. 1976. Theory of the firm: Managerial behavior, agency costs, and owner ship structure. *Journal of Financial Economics*, 3: 305–60.

Johnson, S. G. B., Bilovich, & Tuckett, D. 2023. Conviction narrative theory: A theory of choice under radical uncertainty. *Behavioral and Brain Sciences*, 46. https://doi.org/10.1017/S0140525X22001157.

Joseph, J., & Gaba, V. 2020. Organizational structure, information processing, and decision-making: A retrospective and road map for research. *Academy of Management Annals*, 14: 267–302.

Joseph, J., & Wilson, A. J. 2018. The growth of the firm: An attention-based view. *Strategic Management Journal*, 39: 1779–1800.

Jussim, L. 2012. *Social Perception and Social Reality.* Oxford: Oxford University Press.

Kaczmarek, S., Kimino, S., & Pye, A. 2012. Board task-related faultlines and firm performance: A decade of evidence. *Corporate Governance: An International Review*, 20: 337–351.

Kahneman, D. & Tversky, A. 1979. Prospect theory: An analysis of decision under risk. *Econometrica*, 47: 263–291.

Kahneman, D., & Tversky, A. 1982. The psychology of preferences. *Scientific American*, 246(1): 160–173.

Kahneman, D. 2003. Maps of bounded rationality: Psychology for behavioral economics', *American Economic Review*, 935: 1449–1475.

Kahneman, D. H. 2011. *Thinking Fast and Slow.* London: MacMillan.

Kaplan, R., Schuck, N. W., & Doeller, C. F. 2017. The role of mental maps in decision-making. *Trends in Neurosciences*, 40: 256–259.

Kaplan, S. 2008. Framing contests: Strategy making under uncertainty. *Organization Science*, 19: 729–752.

Kaplan, S. 2011. Research in cognition and strategy: Reflections on two decades of progress and a look to the future. *Journal of Management Studies*, 48(3): 665–695.

Keil, T., Posen, H. E., & Workiewicz, M. 2023. Aspirations, beliefs and a new idea: Building on March's other model of performance feedback. *Academy of Management Review*, 48: 749–771.

Keizer, K., Lindenberg, S. & Steg, L. 2008. The spreading of disorder. *Science*, 322: 1681–1685.

Keizer, K., Lindenberg, S. & Steg, L. 2013. The importance of demonstratively restoring order. *PLoS ONE*, 8: e65137.

Kelly, G. 1970. A brief introduction to personal construct theory. Reprint 2017. *Costruttivismi*, 4: 3–15.

Kemp, A. 2023. Competitive advantages through artificial intelligence: Toward a theory of situated AI. *Academy of Management Review*, in press.

Kiefer, T. 2002. Understanding the emotional experience of organizational change: Evidence from a merger. *Advances in Developing Human Resources*, 4: 39–61.

Kiefer, T. 2005. Feeling bad: Antecedents and consequences of negative emotions in ongoing change. *Journal of Organizational Behavior*, 26: 875–897.

Kiesler, S., & Sproull, L. 1982. Managerial response to changing environments: Perspectives on problem sensing from social cognition. *Administrative Science Quarterly*, 27: 548–570.

Kilduff, G. J. 2019. Interfirm relational rivalry: Implications for competitive strategy. *Academy of Management Review*, 44: 775–799.

Kim, S. 2023. Frame restructuration: The making of an alternative business incubator amid detroit's crisis. *Administrative Science Quarterly*, 66(3): 753–805.

Kogut, B., & Zander, U. 1996. What firms do? Coordination, identity, and learning. *Organization Science*, 7: 502–518.

König, A., Mammen, J., Luger, J., Fehn, A., & Enders, A. 2018. Silver bullet or ricochet? CEOs' use of metaphorical communication and infomediaries' evaluations. *Academy of Management Journal*, 61: 1196–1230.

Kramer, R. M., & Neale, M. A. 1998. *Power and Influence in Organizations*. London: Sage.

Lange, D., Boivie, S., & Westphal, J. D. 2015. Predicting organizational identification at the CEO level. *Strategic Management Journal*, 36: 1224–1244.

Lant, T. K. 1992. Aspiration level adaptation: An empirical exploration. *Management Science*, 38: 623–644.

Lant, T. K., & Mezias, S. J. 1992. An organizational learning model of convergence and reorientation. *Organization Science*, 3: 47–71.

Lau, D. C. and Murnighan, J. K. 1998. Demographic diversity and faultlines: The compositional dynamics of organizational groups. *Academy of Management Review*, 23: 325–40.

Laureiro-Martínez, D., Brusoni, S., & Zollo, M. 2010. The neuroscientific foundations of the exploration–exploitation dilemma. *Journal of Neuroscience, Psychology, and Economics*, 3: 95–115.

Laureiro-Martínez, D., Brusoni, S., Canessa, N., & Zollo, M. 2015. Understanding the exploration–exploitation dilemma: An fMRI study of attention control and decision-making performance. *Strategic Management Journal*, 36: 319–338.

Lawrence, B. S., & Zyphur, M. J. 2011. Identifying organizational faultlines with latent class cluster analysis. *Organizational Research Methods*, 14(1): 32–57.

Leicht-Deobald, U., Huettermann, H., Bruch, H., & Lawrence, B. S. 2021. Organizational demographic faultlines: Their impact on collective organizational identification, firm performance, and firm innovation. *Journal of Management Studies*, 58(8): 2240–2274.

Le Mens, G., Kovács, B., Hannan, M. T., & Pros, G. 2023. Uncovering the semantics of concepts using GPT-4. *Proceedings of the National Academy of Sciences*, 120(49): e2309350120.

Levine, S. S., Schilke, O., Kacperczyk, O., & Zucker, L. G. 2023. Primer for experimental methods in organization theory. *Organization Science*, 34: 1997–2025.

Levinthal, D. A. 1997. Adaptation on rugged landscapes. *Management Science*, 43: 934–950.

Levinthal, D. A. 2011. A behavioral approach to strategy—what's the alternative? *Strategic Management Journal*, 32(13): 1517–1523.

Levinthal, D. A. & March, J. G. 1993. The myopia of learning. *Strategic Management Journal*, 14: 95–112.

Levitt, B., & March, J. G. 1988. Organizational learning. *Annual Review of Sociology*, 14: 319–338.

Levitt, S. D., & List, J. A. 2008. Homo economicus evolves. *Science*, 319: 909–910.

Li, J., & Tang, Y. I. 2010. CEO hubris and firm risk taking in China: The moderating role of managerial discretion. *Academy of Management Journal*, 53(1): 45–68.

Lindebaum, D., Vesa, M., & Den Hond, F. 2020. Insights from "the machine stops" to better understand rational assumptions in algorithmic decision making and its implications for organizations. *Academy of Management Review*, 45(1): 247–263.

Lindenberg, S. & Foss, N. J. 2011 Managing motivation for joint production: The role of goal framing and governance mechanisms. *Academy of Management Review*, 36: 500–525.

Liu, D., Fisher, G., & Chen, G. 2018. CEO attributes and firm performance: A sequential mediation process model. *Academy of Management Annals*, 12: 789–816.

Liu Y. & Perrewé P. 2005. Another look at the role of emotion in the organizational change: A process model. *Human Resource Management Review*, 15(4): 263–280.

Loersch, C., & Payne, B. K. 2014. Situated inferences and the what, who, and where of priming. *Social Cognition*, 32 (Supplement): 137–151.

Lovallo, D. & Sibony, O. 2010. *The Case for Behavioral Strategy: McKinsey Quarterly*. McKinsey: Boston.

Lovallo, D., Clarke, C., & Camerer, C. 2012. Robust analogizing and the outside view: Two empirical tests of case-based decision making. *Strategic Management Journal*, 33: 496–512.

Luan, S., Reb, J., & Gigerenzer, G. (2019). Ecological rationality: Fast-and-frugal heuristics for managerial decision making under uncertainty. *Academy of Management Journal*, 62: 1735–1759.

Luce, R. D., & Raiffa, H. 1957. *Games and Decisions: Introduction and Critical Survey*. New York: Wiley.

Lyles, A. & Schwenk, C. R. 1992. Top management, strategy and organizational knowledge structures. *Journal of Management Studies*, 29: 155–174.

Machlup, F. 1967. Theories of the firm: Marginalist, behavioral, managerial. *American Economic Review*, 57: 1–33.

Mael, F., & Ashforth, B. E. 1992. Alumni and their alma mater: A partial test of the reformulated model of organizational identification. *Journal of organizational Behavior*, 13(2): 103–123.

Maersk. 2023. Annual Report. Accessed June 6, 2024. www.maersk.com

Maitlis, S. 2005. The social processes of organizational sensemaking. *Academy of Management Journal*, 48: 21–49.

Maitlis, S., & Lawrence, T. B. 2007. Triggers and enablers of sensegiving in organizations. *Academy of Management Journal*, 50: 57–84

Maitlis, S., & Sonenshein, S. 2010. Sensemaking in crisis and change: Inspiration and insights from Weick (1988). *Journal of Management Studies*, 47: 551–580.

Mao, A., Chen, Y., Gajos, K. Z. et al. 2012. Turkserver: Enabling synchronous and longitudinal online experiments. *Proceedings of the fourth workshop on human computation*. AAAI Technical Report WS-12–08. https://aaai.org/papers/aaaiw-ws0894-12-5315/.

March, J. G. 1962. The business firm as a political coalition. *Journal of Politics*, 24: 662–678.

March, J. G. 1991. Exploration and exploitation in organizational learning. *Organization Science*, 2: 71–87.

March, J. G., & Olsen, J. P. 1975. The uncertainty of the past: Organizational learning under ambiguity. *European Journal of Political Research*, 3: 147–171.

March, J. G., & Simon, H. A. 1958. *Organizations*. New York: Wiley.

Marchetti, A. & Puranam, P. 2023. Interpreting Topic Models Using Prototypical Text: From "Telling" To "Showing". INSEAD Working Paper No. 2020/49/STR, SSRN: https://ssrn.com/abstract=3717437.

Mayer, K. J., Xing, Z., & Mondal, P. 2022. Contracting for innovation: Designing contracts that account for exchange hazards and the need for innovation. *Strategic Management Journal*, 43: 2253–2278.

Mazzelli, A., Nason, R. S., De Massis, A., & Kotlar, J. 2019. Causality rules: Performance feedback on hierarchically related goals and capital investment variability. *Journal of Management Studies*, 56: 1630–1654.

McDonald, M. L., & Westphal, J. D. 2003. Getting by with the advice of their friends: CEOs' advice networks and firms' strategic responses to poor performance. *Administrative Science Quarterly*, 48: 1–32.

McKee, K. R., Tacchetti, A., Bakker, M. A. et al. 2023. Scaffolding cooperation in human groups with deep reinforcement learning. *Nature Human Behaviour*, 7: 1787–1796.

Mehta, R., & Zhu, R. J. 2009. Blue or red? Exploring the effect of color on cognitive task performances. *Science*, 323: 1226–1229.

Meyer, A. D. 1982. Adapting to environmental jolts. *Administrative Science Quarterly*, 27: 515–537.

Mezias, S. J., & Glynn, M. A. 1993. The three faces of corporate renewal: Institution, revolution, and evolution. *Strategic Management Journal*, 14: 77–101.

Miller, D., & Le Breton–Miller, I. 2011. Governance, social identity, and entrepreneurial orientation in closely held public companies. *Entrepreneurship Theory and Practice*, 35: 1051–1076.

Miller, D., Le Breton-Miller, I., & Lester, R. H. 2011. Family and lone founder ownership and strategic behaviour: Social context, identity, and institutional logics. *Journal of Management Studies*, 48: 1–25.

Mintzberg, H., Raisinghani, D., & Theoret, A. 1976. The structure of "unstructured" decision processes. *Administrative Science Quarterly*, 246–275.

Mithani, M. A., & O'Brien, J. P. 2021. So what exactly is a "coalition" within an organization? A review and organizing framework. *Journal of Management*, 47: 171–206.

Monin, P., Noorderhaven, N., Vaara, E., & Kroon, D. 2013. Giving sense to and making sense of justice in postmerger integration. *Academy of Management Journal*, 56(1): 256–284.

Mousavi, S. & Gigerenzer, G. 2014. Risk, uncertainty, and heuristics. *Journal of Business Research*, 67: 1671–1678.

Murray, A., Rhymer, J. E. N., & Sirmon, D. G. 2021. Humans and technology: Forms of conjoined agency in organizations. *Academy of Management Review*, 46(3): 552–571.

Nadkarni, S., & Chen, J. 2014. Bridging yesterday, today, and tomorrow: CEO temporal focus, environmental dynamism, and rate of new product introduction. *Academy of Management Journal*, 57: 1810–1833.

Nag, R., Corley, K. G., & Gioia, D. A. 2007. The intersection of organizational identity, knowledge, and practice: Attempting strategic change via knowledge grafting. *Academy of Management Journal*, 50: 821–847.

Nason, R. S., Bacq, S., & Gras, D. 2018. A behavioral theory of social performance: Social identity and stakeholder expectations. *Academy of Management Review*, 43(2): 259–283.

Nason, R., Mazzelli, A., & Carney, M. 2019. The ties that unbind: Socialization and business-owning family reference point shift. *Academy of Management Review*, 44: 846–870.

Nayak, A., Chia, R., & Canales, J. I. 2020. Noncognitive microfoundations: Understanding dynamic capabilities as idiosyncratically refined sensitivities and predispositions. *Academy of Management Review*, 45: 280–303.

Neumann, J. von & Morgenstern, O. 1944. *Theory of Games and Economic Behavior*. Princeton: Princeton University Press.

Ndofor, H. A., Sirmon, D. G., & He, X. 2015. Utilizing the firm's resources: How TMT heterogeneity and resulting faultlines affect TMT tasks. *Strategic Management Journal*, 36: 1656–1674.

Nelson, R. R., & Winter, S. G. 1982. The Schumpeterian tradeoff revisited. *American Economic Review*, 72: 114–132.

Newell, A., Shaw, J. C., & Simon, H. A. 1958. Elements of a theory of human problem solving. *Psychological Review*, 65: 151–166.

Newell, A., & Simon, H. A. 1972. *Human Problem Solving*. Englewood Cliffs, NJ: Prentice-Hall.

Nickerson, J. A., Silverman, B. S., & Zenger, T. R. 2007. The problem of creating and capturing value. *Strategic Organization*, 5: 211–225.

Nickerson, J. A., & Zenger, T. R. 2008. Envy, comparison costs, and the economic theory of the firm. *Strategic Management Journal*, 29: 1429–1449.

Nilsson, N. J. 1971. *Problem-solving Methods in Artificial Intelligence*. New York: McGraw-Hill Book.

Obel, B., & Burton, R. M. 1984. *Designing Efficient Organizations: Modelling and Experimentation*. North-Holland: Amsterdam.

Ocasio, W. 1997. Towards an attention-based view of the firm. *Strategic Management Journal*, 18: 187–206.

Ocasio, W. (2011). Attention to attention. *Organization Science*, 22(5): 1286–1296.

Ocasio, W., & Joseph, J. 2005. An attention-based theory of strategy formulation: Linking micro-and macroperspectives in strategy processes. In G. Szulanski, J. Porac, & Y. Doz (eds.), *Strategy Process* (pp. 39–61). Leeds, England: Emerald Group.

Ocasio, W., & Joseph, J. 2008. Rise and fall or transformation?: The evolution of strategic planning at the General Electric Company, 1940–2006. *Long Range Planning*, 41: 248–272.

Oeberst, A. & Imhoff, R. 2023. Toward parsimony in bias research: A proposed common framework of belief-consistent information processing for a set of biases. *Perspectives on Psychological Science*, 18(6): 1464–1487. https://journals.sagepub.com/doi/epub/10.1177/17456916221148147.

Ouchi, W. G. 1980. Markets, bureaucracies, and clans. *Administrative Science Quarterly*, 25(1): 129–141.

Ouchi, W. G., & Barney, J. B. 1980. *Efficient Boundaries*. Mimeographed. Los Angeles: University of California, Los Angeles.

Paolacci, G., Chandler, J., & Ipeirotis, P. G. 2010. Running experiments on amazon mechanical turk. *Judgment and Decision Making*, 5: 411–419.

Parker, S. C., & Witteloostuijn, A. V. 2010. A general framework for estimating multidimensional contingency fit. *Organization Science*, 21: 540–553.

Parmigiani, A. & Howard-Grenville, J. 2011. Routines revisited: Exploring the capabilities and practice perspectives. *Academy of Management Annals*, 5: 413–453.

Penrose, E. T. 1959. *The Theory of the Growth of the Firm.* Oxford: Oxford University Press.

Pentland, B. T., Feldman, M. S., Becker, M. C. and Liu, P. 2012. Dynamics of organizational routines: A generative model. *Journal of Management Studies*, 49: 1484–1508.

Pepper, A., & Gore, J. 2015. Behavioral agency theory: New foundations for theorizing about executive compensation. *Journal of Management*, 41: 1045–1068.

Pepper, A., Gosling, T., & Gore, J. 2015. Fairness, envy, guilt and greed: Building equity considerations into agency theory. *Human Relations*, 68: 1291–1314.

Perrow, C. 1984. *Normal Accidents: Living with High-Risk Technologies.* New York: Basic Books.

Pfarrer, M. D., Devers, C. E., Corley, K. et al. 2019. Sociocognitive perspectives in strategic management. *Academy of Management Review*, 44: 767–774.

Piezunka, H., Aggarwal, V. A., & Posen, H. E. 2022. The aggregation–learning trade-off. *Organization Science*, 33: 1094–1115.

Piezunka, H., & Dahlander, L. 2015. Distant search, narrow attention: How crowding alters organizations' filtering of suggestions in crowdsourcing. *Academy of Management Journal*, 58: 856–880.

Piezunka, H., & Schilke, O. 2023. The dual function of organizational structure: Aggregating and shaping individuals' votes. *Organization Science*, 34(5): 1651–1996.

Porac, J. F., Thomas, H., & Baden-Fuller, C. 1989. Competitive groups as cognitive communities: The case of Scottish knitwear manufacturers. *Journal of Management Studies*, 26(4): 397–416.

Porac, J. F., Thomas, H., Wilson, F., Paton, D., & Kanfer, A. 1995. Rivalry and the industry model of Scottish Knitwear producers. *Administrative Science Quarterly*, 40: 203–227.

Porter, M. E. 1980. Industry structure and competitive strategy: Keys to profitability. *Financial Analysts Journal*, 36: 30–41.

Posen, H. E., Keil, T., Kim, S., & Meissner, F. D. 2018. Renewing research on problemistic search—A review and research agenda. *Academy of Management Annals*, 12(1): 208–251.

Powell, T. C., Lovallo, D., & Fox, C. R. 2011. Behavioral strategy. *Strategic Management Journal*, 32: 1369–1386.

Prasad, A., & Prasad, P. 2002. The coming of age of interpretive organizational research. *Organizational Research Methods*, 5: 4–11.

Prinz, K. 2022. *The Smiling Chatbot: Investigating Emotional Contagion in Human-to-Chatbot Service Interactions.* Koblenz: Springer Nature.

Puranam, P., Stieglitz, N. Osman, M., & Pillutla, M. 2015. Modelling bounded rationality in organizations: Progress and prospects. *Academy of Management Annals*, 9: 337–392.

Rafaeli, A. & Worline, M. 2001. Individual emotion in work organizations. *Social Science Information*, 40: 95–123.

Raisch, S., & Krakowski, S. 2021. Artificial intelligence and management: The automation–augmentation paradox. *Academy of Management Review*, 46: 192–210.

Rand, D. G. 2012. The promise of Mechanical Turk: How online labor markets can help theorists run behavioral experiments. *Journal of Theoretical Biology*, 299: 172–179.

Ravasi, D., & Schultz, M. 2006. Responding to organizational identity threats: Exploring the role of organizational culture. *Academy of Management Journal*, 4: 433–458.

Reger, R. K., & Huff, A. S. 1993. Strategic groups: A cognitive perspective. *Strategic Management Journal*, 14: 103–123.

Reger, R., Mullane, J., Gustafson, L. et al. 1994. Creating earthquakes to change organizational mindsets. *Academy of Management Executive*, 8: 31–46.

Reinholt, M., Pedersen, T., & Foss, N. J. 2011. Why a central network position isn't enough: The moderating roles of motivation and ability for knowledge sharing in employee networks. *Academy of Management Journal*, 54: 1277–1297.

Rhee, M., Kim, Y. C., & Han, J. 2006. Confidence in imitation: Niche-width strategy in the UK automobile industry. *Management Science*, 52: 501–513.

Riessman, C. K. 1993. *Narrative Analysis*. Newbury Park, CA: Sage.

Rindova, V. P., & Fombrun, C. J. 1999. Constructing competitive advantage: the role of firm–constituent interactions. *Strategic Management Journal*, 20: 691–710.

Rindova, V. P., & Martins, L. L. 2021. Shaping possibilities: A design science approach to developing novel strategies. *Academy of Management Review*, 46: 800–822.

Rindova, V. P., & Martins, L. L. 2022. Futurescapes: Imagination and temporal reorganization in the design of strategic narratives. *Strategic Organization*, 20: 200–224.

Rindova, V. P., Reger, R. K., & Dalpiaz, E. 2012. The mind of the strategist and the eye of the beholder: The socio-cognitive perspective in strategy research. In G. B. Dagnino (eds.), *Handbook of Research on Competitive Strategy* (pp. 147–164). Cheltenham, UK: Edgar Elgar.

Riordan, M. H., & Williamson, O. E. 1985. Asset specificity and economic organization. *International Journal of Industrial Organization*, 3: 365–378.

Rumelt, R. P. 1979. Evaluation of strategies: Theory and models. In D. E. Schendel, & C. W. Hofer (eds.), *Strategic Management: A New View of Business Policy and Planning* (pp. 196–212). Boston: Little, Brown.

Sacks, H. 1966. *Lectures on Conversation, vol. I.* Malden, MA: Blackwell.

Sah, R. K. & Stiglitz, J. E. 1986. The architecture of economic systems: Hierarchies and polyarchies. *American Economic Review*, 76: 716–727.

Schiller, D., Eichenbaum, H., Buffalo, E. A. et al. 2015. Memory and space: Towards an understanding of the cognitive map. *Journal of Neuroscience*, 35: 13904–13911.

Schilling, M. A. 2018. The cognitive foundations of visionary strategy. *Strategy Science*, 3: 335–342.

Schwenk, C. R. 1984. Cognitive simplification processes in strategic decision-making. *Strategic Management Journal*, 5: 111–128.

Sebhatu, A., Wennberg, K., Arora-Jonsson, S., & Lindberg, S. 2020. Explaining the homogeneous diffusion of COVID-19 nonpharmaceutical interventions across heterogeneous countries. *PNAS*, 117: 21201–21208.

Semadeni, M., Chin, M. K., & Krause, R. 2022. Pumping the brakes: Examining the impact of CEO political ideology divergence on firm responses. *Academy of Management Journal*, 65: 516–544.

Sent, E. M. 2004. Behavioral economics: How psychology made its (limited) way back into economics. *History of Political Economy*, 36: 735–760.

Shirado, H. & Christakis, N. A. 2020. Network engineering using autonomous agents increases cooperation in human groups. *iScience*, 23: 101438.

Simon, H. A. 1947. *Administrative Behavior: A Study of Decision-Making Processes in Administrative Organization.* 1st ed. New York: Macmillan.

Simon, H. A. 1947. *Administrative Behavior: A Study of Decision-Making Processes in Administrative Organizations.* 2nd ed. New York: Macmillan.

Simon, H. A. 1967. Motivational and emotional controls of cognition. *Psychological Review*, 74: 29–39.

Simon, H. A. 1955. A behavioral model of rational choice. *Quarterly Journal of Economics*, 69: 99–118.

Simon, H. A. 1956. Rational choice and the structure of the environment. *Psychological Review*, 63: 129–138.

Simon, H. A. 1978. Rationality as process and as product of thought. *American Economic Review*, 68: 1–16.

Simon, H. A. 1985. Human nature in politics: The dialogue of psychology with political science. *American Political Science Review*, 79(2): 293–304.

Simon, H. A. 1991. Organizations and markets. *Journal of Economic Perspectives*, 5: 25–44.

Simon, H. A., & Newell, A. 1971. Human problem solving: The state of the theory in 1970. *American Psychologist*, 26: 145–159.

Simon, H. A., & Newell, A. 1976. Computer science as empirical inquiry: Symbols and search. *Communications of the Association for Computing Machinery*, 19(3): 11–126.

Simsek, Z., Heavey, C., & Fox, B. C. 2018. Interfaces of strategic leaders: A conceptual framework, review, and research agenda. *Journal of Management*, 44: 280–324.

Sonenshein, S. 2010. We're changing—Or are we? Untangling the role of progressive, regressive, and stability narratives during strategic change implementation. *Academy of Management Journal*, 53: 477–512.

Spender, J. C. 1989. *Industry Recipes: An Enquiry into the Nature and Sources of Managerial Judgement*. Oxford, UK: Blackwell.

Spiliopoulos, L., & Hertwig, R. 2023. Variance, skewness and multiple outcomes in described and experienced prospects: Can one descriptive model capture it all? *Journal of Experimental Psychology: General*, 152: 1188–1222.

Stachenfeld, K. L., Botvinick, M. M., & Gershman, S. J. 2017. The hippocampus as a predictive map. *Nature Neuroscience*, 20: 1643–1653.

Starbuck, W. H., & Milliken, F. J. 1988. Executive's perceptual filters: What they notice and how they make sense. In D. Hambrick (ed.), The Executive Effect: Concepts and Methods for Studying Top Managers, pp. 35-66. Greenwich, CT: JAI Press.

Staw, B. M., & Ross, J. 1980. Commitment in an experimenting society: A study of the attribution of leadership from administrative scenarios. *Journal of Applied Psychology*, 65: 249–260.

Steinbach, A. L., Gamache, D. L., & Johnson, R. E. 2019. Don't get it misconstrued: Executive construal-level shifts and flexibility in the upper echelons. *Academy of Management Review*, 44(4), 871–895.

Stevenson, W. B., & Greenberg, D. 2000. Agency and social networks: Strategies of action in a social structure of position, opposition, and opportunity. *Administrative Science Quarterly*, 45: 651–678.

Stoewer, P., Schilling, A., Maier, A., & Krauss, P. 2023. Neural network based formation of cognitive maps of semantic spaces and the putative emergence of abstract concepts. *Scientific Reports*, 13: 3644.

Strike, V. M., & Rerup, C. 2016. Mediated sensemaking. *Academy of Management Journal*, 59: 880–905.

Sutcliffe, K. M. 2013 Sensemaking. In M. Augier and D. Teece (eds.), *Palgrave Encyclopedia of Strategic Management* (pp. 1–4). Palgrave Macmillan: London.

Taleb, N. N. 2007. Black swans and the domains of statistics. *The American Statistician*, 61: 198–200.

Tajfel, H. 1978. *Differentiation between Social Groups: Studies in the Social Psychology of Intergroup Relations*. London: Academic.

Tajfel, H. & Turner, J. C. 1986. The social identity theory of intergroup behaviour. In S. Worchel, & W. G. Austin (eds.), *Psychology of Intergroup Relations* (pp. 7–24). Chicago: Nelson-Hall.

Tasselli, S., Kilduff, M., & Menges, J. I. 2015. The microfoundations of organizational social networks: A review and an agenda for future research. *Journal of Management*, 41: 1361–1387.

Terry, D. J., & Hogg, M. A. 1996. Group norms and the attitude-behavior relationship: A role for group identification. *Personality and Social Psychology Bulletin*, 22(8): 776–793.

Thatcher, S. M. B., & Patel, P. C. 2012. Group faultlines: A review, integration, and guide to future research. *Journal of Management*, 38: 969–1009.

Thomas, J. B., Clark, S. M., & Gioia, D. A. 1993. Strategic sensemaking and organizational performance: Linkages among scanning, interpretation, action, and outcomes. *Academy of Management Journal*, 36: 239–270.

Thomas, J. B., Sussman, S. W., & Henderson, J. C. 2001. Understanding "strategic learning": Linking organizational learning, knowledge management, and sensemaking. *Organization Science*, 12: 331–345.

Thompson, R. F. 1967. *Foundations of Physiological Psychology*. New York: Harper and Row.

Thorngate, W. 1976. Possible limits on a science of social behavior. In L. H. Strickland, F. E. Aboud, K. J. Gergen (eds.), *Social Psychology in Transition* (pp. 121–139). Boston, MA: Springer US.

Tolman, E. C. 1948. Cognitive maps in rats and men. *Psychological Review*, 55: 189–208.

Tong, S., Jia, N., Luo, X., & Fang, Z. 2021. The Janus face of artificial intelligence feedback: Deployment versus disclosure effects on employee performance. *Strategic Management Journal*, 42: 1600–1631.

Tripsas, M. & Gavetti, G. 2000. Capabilities, cognition, and inertia: Evidence from digital imaging. *Strategic Management Journal*, 21(10/11): 1147–1161.

Tsay, C. J. 2021. Visuals dominate investor decisions about entrepreneurial pitches. *Academy of Management Discoveries*, 7(3): 343–366.

Tsvetkova, M. & Macy, M. W. 2015. The social contagion of antisocial behavior. *Sociological Science*, 2: 36–49.

Tuggle, C. S., Schnatterly, K., & Johnson, R. A. 2010. Attention patterns in the boardroom: How board composition and processes affect discussion of entrepreneurial issues. *Academy of Management Journal*, 53: 550–571.

Tushman, M. L., & Nadler, D. A. 1978. Information processing as an integrating concept in organizational design. *Academy of Management Review*, 3: 613–624.

Tversky, A., & Fox, C. R. 1995. Weighing risk and uncertainty. *Psychological Review*, 102: 269.

Tversky, A., & Kahneman, D. 1974. Judgment under uncertainty: Heuristics and biases. *Science*, 185: 1124–1131.

Tversky, A. & Wakker, P. 1995. Risk attitudes and decision weights. *Econometrica*, 63: 1255–1280

Tversky, B. 1974. Eye fixations in prediction of recognition and recall. *Memory & Cognition*, 2: 275–278.

Van Knippenberg, D. & Van Kleef, G. A. 2016. Leadership and affect: Moving the hearts and minds of followers. *Academy of Management Annals*, 10(1): 799–840.

Veblen, T. 1898. Why is economics not an evolutionary science? *Quarterly Journal of Economics*, 12: 373–397.

Vissa, B. 2010. A matching theory of entrepreneurs' tie formation intentions and initiation of economic exchange. *Academy of Management Journal*, 54: 137–158.

Visser, V., van Knippenberg D., Van Kleef G. A., Wisse B. 2013. How leader displays of happiness and sadness influence follower performance: Emotional contagion and creative versus analytical performance. *Leadership Quarterly*, 24: 172–188.

Von Krogh, G. 2018. Artificial intelligence in organizations: New opportunities for phenomenon-based theorizing. *Academy of Management Discoveries*, 4(4): 404–409.

Vuori, T. O., & Huy, Q. N. 2020. Regulating top managers' emotions during strategy making: Nokia's socially distributed approach enabling radical change from mobile phones to networks in 2007–2013. *Academy of Management Journal*, 65: 331–361.

Wade, J. B., Porac, J. F., & Pollock, T. G. 1997. Worth, words, and the justification of executive pay. *Journal of Organizational Behavior: The International Journal of Industrial, Occupational and Organizational Psychology and Behavior*, 18: 641–664.

Walker, M. H., & Lynn, F. B. 2013. The embedded self: A social networks approach to identity theory. *Social Psychology Quarterly*, 76: 151–179.

Walsh, J. P. 1995. Managerial and organizational cognition: Notes from a trip down memory lane. *Organization Science*, 6: 280–321.

Walsh, J. P., & Fahey, L. 1986. The role of negotiated belief structures in strategy making. *Journal of Management*, 12: 325–338.

Wang, H., Jia, M., Xiang, Y., & Lan, Y. 2022. Social performance feedback and firm communication strategy. *Journal of Management*, 48: 2382–2420.

Watson, T. J. 2009. Narrative, life story and manager identity: A case study in autobiographical identity work. *Human relations*, 62: 425–452.

Weber, J. M., & Murnighan, J. K. 2008. Suckers or saviors? Consistent contributors in social dilemmas. *Journal of Personality and Social Psychology*, 95: 1340–1353.

Weber, L. 2017. A sociocognitive view of repeated interfirm exchanges: How the coevolution of trust and learning impacts subsequent contracts. *Organization Science*, 28: 744–759.

Weber, L. & Bauman, C. W. 2019. The cognitive and behavioral impact of promotion and prevention contracts on trust in repeated exchanges. *Academy of Management Journal*, 62: 361–382.

Weber, L. & Coff, R. 2023. Managers' perceptions and microfoundations of contract design. *Academy of Management Review*, in press.

Weber, L., & Mayer, K. J. 2011. Designing effective contracts: Exploring the influence of framing and expectations. *Academy of Management Review*, 36: 53–75.

Weber, L., & Mayer, K. J. 2014. Transaction cost economics and the cognitive perspective: Investigating the sources and governance of interpretive uncertainty. *Academy of Management Review*, 39(3): 344–363.

Weber, L., Mayer, K. J., & Macher, J. T. 2011. An analysis of extendibility and early termination provisions: The importance of framing duration safeguards. *Academy of Management Journal*, 54: 182–202.

Weber, L., Foss, N. J., & Lindenberg, S. 2023. The role of cognition and motivation in understanding internal governance and hierarchical failure: A discriminating alignment analysis. *Academy of Management Review*, 48: 244–263.

Weick, K. E. 1979. *The Social Psychology of Organizing*, 2d ed. New York: Random House.

Weick, K. E. 1988. Enacted sensemaking in crisis situations. *Journal of Management Studies*, 25: 305–317.

Weick K. E. 1993. Organizational redesign as improvisation. In G. P. Huber and W. H. Glick (eds.), *Organizational Change and Redesign* (pp. 346–79). Oxford University Press: New York.

Weick, K. E. 1995. *Sensemaking in Organizations*. Thousand Oaks, CA: Sage.

Weick, K. E. 2005. Organizing and failures of imagination. *International Public Management Journal*, 8: 425–438.

Weick, K. E. 2010. Reflections on enacted sensemaking in the Bhopal disaster. *Journal of Management Studies*, 47: 537–550.

Weick, K. E., & Roberts, K. H. 1993. Collective mind in organizations: Heedful interrelating on flight decks. *Administrative Science Quarterly*, 38: 357–381.

Wesley, C. L., Martin, G. W., Rice, D. B., & Lubojacky, C. J. 2022. Do the right thing: The imprinting of deonance at the upper echelons. *Journal of Business Ethics*, 180: 187–213.

Westphal, J. D., & Zajac, E. J. 2013. A behavioral theory of corporate governance: Explicating the mechanisms of socially situated and socially constituted agency. *Academy of Management Annals*, 7: 607–661.

Whetten, D. A. 2006. Albert and Whetten revisited: Strengthening the concept of organizational identity. *Journal of Management Inquiry*, 15: 219–234.

Williamson, O. E. 1975. *Markets and Hierarchies: Analysis and Antitrust Implications*. New York: The Free Press.

Williamson, O. E. 1985. *The Economic Institutions of Capitalism*. New York: Free Press.

Williamson, O. E. 1991. Comparative economic organization: The analysis of discrete structural alternatives. *Administrative Science Quarterly*, 36: 269–296.

Williamson, O. E. 1993. Opportunism and its critics. *Managerial and Decision Economics*, 14(2): 97–107.

Williamson, O. E. 1996. *The Mechanisms of Governance*. Oxford: Oxford university press.

Winter, S. G. 2012. Purpose and progress in the theory of strategy: Comments on Gavetti. *Organization Science*, 23(1): 288–297.

Wiseman, R. M., & Gomez-Mejia, L. R. 1998. A behavioral agency model of managerial risk taking. *Academy of Management Review*, 23: 133–153.

Wodak, R., Kwon, W., & Clarke, I. 2011. "Getting people on board": Discursive leadership for consensus building in team meetings. *Discourse & Society*, 22: 592–644.

Wu, J., Liden, R. C., Liao, C., & Wayne, S. J. 2021. Does manager servant leadership lead to follower serving behaviors? It depends on follower self-interest. *Journal of Applied Psychology*, 106: 152–167.

Cambridge Elements ᵓ

Business Strategy

J.-C. Spender
Kozminski University

J.-C. Spender is a research Professor, Kozminski University. He has been active in the
business strategy field since 1971 and is the author or co-author of 7 books and
numerous papers. His principal academic interest is in knowledge-based theories of the
private sector firm, and managing them.

Advisory Board

About the Series

Business strategy's reach is vast, and important too since wherever there is business
activity there is strategizing. As a field, strategy has a long history from medieval and
colonial times to today's developed and developing economies. This series offers
a place for interesting and illuminating research including industry and
corporate studies, strategizing in service industries, the arts, the public sector, and the
new forms of Internet-based commerce. It also covers today's expanding
gamut of analytic techniques.

Cambridge Elements ≡

Business Strategy

Elements in the Series

Printed in the United States
by Baker & Taylor Publisher Services